Praise for *Sweep*

"Gary Thorp has discovered joy and fulfillment in everyday tasks, [which is] both an inspiration and a challenge. We too have the potential to come alive through the ordinary."

—Edward Espé Brown, author of *Tomato Blessings and Radish Teachings* and *The Tassajara Bread Book*

"Gary Thorp's pliant, lean book is about how to intimately live with your (homeless) home. Everybody needs to read it! Zen teachers here and there through the centuries have said that tiles, fence posts, and faucets are constantly presenting the Dharma. Thorp's book tells us how to begin to hear them."

—Gary Snyder, author of *The Practice of the Wild*

"This elegant, warmhearted little treatise is brimming with a kind of simple wisdom that so eludes our modern, linear thinking. I'm grateful to Gary Thorp for showing us, with his clear voice and gentle, compassionate humor, that there is holiness in the mundane. 'Cleaning,' then, becomes not a chore, but a cleansing, a pathway to increased relaxation and deeper, more meaningful function."

—Mollie Katzen, author of *The Moosewood Cookbook*

"Enlightening . . . a very fine example of everyday spirituality."

—*Spirituality and Health*

"[Thorp] shows us that the opportunity to live richly and fully is everywhere—in the dirty toilet and in the refrigerator that needs to be cleaned out."

—*San Jose Mercury News*

BROADWAY BOOKS
NEW YORK

Sweeping Changes

DISCOVERING
THE JOY OF ZEN
IN EVERYDAY TASKS

Gary Thorp

BROADWAY

A hardcover edition of this book was originally published in 2000 by Walker & Company. It is here reprinted by arrangement with Walker & Company.

Walker & Company
435 Hudson Street
New York, NY 10014

Broadway Books titles may be purchased for business or promotional use or for special sales. For information, please write to: Special Markets Department, Random House, Inc., 1540 Broadway, New York, NY 10036.

BROADWAY BOOKS and its logo, a letter B bisected on the diagonal, are trademarks of Broadway Books, a division of Random House, Inc.

Visit our website at www.broadwaybooks.com

First Broadway Books trade paperback edition published 2001.

Library of Congress Cataloging-in-Publication Data

Thorp, Gary.
    Sweeping changes: discovering the joy of Zen in
      everyday tasks / Gary Thorp.
        p.   cm.
    Originally published: New York: Walker & Company, Inc. 2000.
    Includes bibliographical references and index.
    1. Religious life—Zen Buddhism. I. Title.

BQ9286 .T56 2001
294.3'4446—dc21   2001035252

The quotations on pages 4 and 26 are reprinted from *Zen Mind, Beginner's Mind* by Shunryu Suzuki Roshi with permission of Weatherhill, Trumbull, Connecticut.
The quotation on page 142 is reprinted from *Fragrant Palm Leaves: Journals 1962–1966* (1998) by Thich Nhat Hanh with permission of Parallax Press, Berkeley, California.

ISBN 0-7679-0773-6

10 9 8 7 6 5 4 3 2 1

This housecleaning day . . .

All gods and buddhas are left

sitting out on the grass.

—Masaoka Shiki

Contents

Acknowledgments

As the Zen poet Ryokan said, "In this one bowl, there is rice from a thousand households." This book could not have been written without the interest and support of my family, friends, fellow students, and teachers. I am grateful to my first teacher, Wako Kazumitsu Kato, who pointed me toward the right path, and to the following teachers and friends who, either through great effort or with just a few well-chosen words, helped nudge me along my way: Gary Snyder; the legacies of Shunryo Suzuki Roshi and Dainin Katagiri Roshi; Tenshin Reb Anderson, Zoketsu Norman Fischer, Meiya Wender, Taigen Dan Leighton, and the many other teachers and students at Green Gulch Farm Zen Center, Tassajara Zen Mountain Center, and the San Francisco Zen Center.

I would also like to offer my deep appreciation and sincere thanks to my current teacher, Jusan Edward Espe Brown, who keeps the dharma simmering, as bubbling and alive as any of his good soups, and to the sometimes rowdy group of sitters in Edward's Thursday evening *sangha*: George Lane, Betsy Bryant, Ginny Stanford, Hermann Clasen, Anne K. Brown, Harriette Greene, Peter Elias, and Patricia Sullivan, to name just a few.

Thanks, also, to literary agent and longtime friend Victoria Shoemaker, and to my editor at Walker & Company, Jackie Johnson, and copyeditor Vicki Haire. Their skill and patience and dedication to their work are models for all of us to follow, and this book would not exist without their help. Any remaining errors are, of course, my own.

Finally, I would like to thank my wife, Lura, for her love, patience, support, and companionship all these years and especially during the writing of this book. The ways in which she enriches my life are limitless.

foreword

EDWARD ESPE BROWN

My first encounter with Zen cleaning was at Zen Center in San Francisco, in 1965. After meditation and breakfast on Saturday mornings, we had a work period. No one explained what should be done or who was to do what. Everyone else seemed to know without being told. People began washing and drying the dishes; scrubbing, waxing, and polishing the zendo (meditation hall) floor; cleaning the bathrooms.

I looked around and wondered what to do. It seemed as if all the possible jobs were being done. I was puzzled at how to join the party, and since the whole event happened in silence, I couldn't ask anyone. I had to figure it out for myself and just plunge in—if not the first time, then certainly the next. Maybe I could get to the dishes before someone else!

Although the process was initially daunting, over time it came to seem quite natural and uplifting. No one was bossing around anyone else, as though some knew exactly what to do and others needed to be told. The unspoken message was that everyone was capable of participating; everyone was capable of figuring out what to do and how to do it; everyone was competent. You simply joined in.

Still, my favorite part of the work period was observing the manner in which one of our teachers, Katagiri Roshi, tackled his jobs. It was a joy to see, for example, the energy flowing through him as he applied paste wax to the zendo floor. How could waxing the floor be that important? Yet there he was, devoting himself to this mundane task. Next came the arduous, almost acrobatic act of polishing, which no one else seemed able to perform with quite the same grace and verve. Bent over with both hands on the polishing cloth, Katagiri Roshi would run from one end of the zendo to the other, pause briefly, and then run back. The movements were graceful, natural, unaffected.

I felt happy and inspired, seeing that this person was not above work, work with his body, work with his hands—cleaning work. Equally inspiring was to see and feel the robustness of his effort, the completeness, the joy. As he would sometimes say in later years, "The meaning of life is to live," and "Let the flower of your life force bloom." Few people, in my opinion, have *lived* floor polishing the way he did.

Of course, this experience was just part of the equation, but I ended up living at Zen Center for perhaps twenty years. The regularity of life, the daily ritual was both comforting and reassuring, and the practice of cleaning continued to be an essential element: "Zen is meditation and sweeping the garden." And there's no telling how big your garden is.

When we first arrived at Tassajara Hot Springs to begin our monastery there, our teacher, Suzuki Roshi, noticed a broom leaning against a wall, bristles down, and he commented on how the bristles were curled way over to one side, making the broom rather difficult to use effectively. "Put the broom away with its bristles facing up," he said. "This way the bristles will not get bent over. This will be our first rule here at Tassajara."

Every fifth day we had a lighter schedule of meditation. Our teachers were careful about language, so they cautioned us not to call it "a day off." "There are no days 'off' in Zen," they would say. "Every day is a good day." So we called them by their traditional name, "four and nine days" (all calendar days that contain either a four or a nine).

These were days to do one's wash—labor-intensive hand-scrubbing and wringer-twisting—and the sewing, to mend the rips and tears, the frayed edges. Of course, there were other frayed edges that we mended with sleep. In midafternoon we had community cleanup, followed by forty-five minutes of room cleaning.

The general community pickup and scrubdown included raking the grounds and cleaning the public bathrooms, the latter accomplished by the head monk, emblematic of the Zen way. "The higher you go, the more excrement you are willing to clean up." Spiritual virtue accumulates through spiritual servitude.

I cleaned my room religiously, even though some students disappeared during that "private" time. Most satisfying was mopping the wooden floor with a damp rag after sweeping. While doing this activity, I chanted a mantra I made up: "Get in the corners. Get in the grooves. Get out the dirt. Get out the blues." Empty the trash. Remove the debris. For a few minutes each week, cleaning my room was the assigned spiritual practice. What a surprise. And what a gift to be given and to give myself.

Once the grounds were tidied and our rooms cleaned, we bathed ourselves in the hot tubs, dressed in our fresh robes, and assembled outside the meditation hall. After chanting, we entered ceremonially, honoring our leaders, our ancestors, and one another by bowing. Life was new and fresh, and we were ready to go again.

Sometimes we would question our teachers: "Isn't dirt as holy as clean?" "Isn't sound as sacred as silence?" And they would explain: "We don't clean in order to clean. It is a way of practicing respect for things. More simply, it is a way for us to spend time together, and spending time together, we realize our interconnectedness. Otherwise we take things for granted.

"When we clean we begin to appreciate how things are there for us, supporting us, encouraging us, and when we appreciate things we appreciate ourselves and one another. So to respect the floor or the grounds is to respect ourselves. This is how we develop intimacy and connection. Although everything is one, you will not understand what that means unless you practice it. When you clean, you experience the oneness. You realize everything is helping you.

"Not concerning yourself with the care of things may, on the surface, seem to be desirable but, in this context, it is considered lazy and self-centered, as if you are trying to exist apart from things. That's one of the reasons you feel disconnected and unsupported."

Each day someone was assigned to tend the meditation hall, to offer one's presence. Much of the time would be spent cleaning: sweeping (with a variety of brooms, each with a designated purpose) the round cushions, the flat cushions, the raised wooden platform, the floor; wet-mopping, waxing, and polishing the floor. And the kerosene lamps needed to be cleaned and filled. Before starting in the morning, I would view the cleaning ahead as a dreary time, but by the end of the day I knew differently: I belong here because I clean here. I am supported; I am welcome here when I touch these places with devotion and kind attention.

Since moving out of Zen Center, I haven't done very well at keeping up with my Zen cleaning practice, so my house is rather messy. The lived-in quality is not something I hide. I don't mind people visiting and seeing the debris. Sometimes they express surprise or even disillusionment that a Zen teacher would live as I do. "This isn't my idea of a Zen house," they say.

(On the other hand, some appear relieved not to have yet another high standard to live up to.) I live a life that works for me, and then again it doesn't. So I continue to examine the way I live and investigate alternatives.

If I want to rationalize the disarray in which I live, I tell people, "I'm an artist." Zen, it seems, has not yet arrived at my house, and I haven't figured out what to do with all the books, papers, computers, photos, cards . . . and stuff keeps arriving.

Recently, the manuscript for Gary Thorp's *Sweeping Changes* came in the mail. I found it to be sweet and endearing, alternately intoxicating and sobering. That Gary has discovered joy and fulfillment in everyday tasks is both an inspiration and a challenge. For his message is that we all have the potential to come alive through the ordinary, rather than waiting for something extraordinary to awaken our energy and passion. After I read Gary's manuscript, the first thing I wanted to do was tidy up. My latent housekeeping impulse went right to work. Then I returned to writing or brooding. Inspiration is everywhere, right at hand, whenever I choose to reach out. But that doesn't mean that I do.

Liberation means we do not stick to anything, whether it is messiness or cleanliness. We keep finding out how to live and realize that we have limitless choices.

Gil Fronsdal, who is both a Zen priest and a Vipassana (insight meditation) teacher, once spoke of practicing Zen in Japan and Vipassana in Southeast Asia. "Everyone," he said, "loves to rake." In Japan the advice is "When you rake, just rake," whereas in Southeast Asia it's "When you rake, watch your mind." So the monks in Japan work with energetic focus (sometimes stirring up unruly dust), while their counterparts can sometimes be found barely moving their rakes, being so watchful of feelings, thoughts, motives, intentions, sensations, emotions. When I told Mel Weitsman, another Zen teacher, about the Vipassana approach, his terse but amusing comment was, "They still think their minds are in their heads."

How will we spend our too-short lives?

In everything we do we are expressing ourselves and revealing ourselves, if we care to look. When several of us from Zen Center went with Suzuki Roshi to practice a day of meditation at an alternative high school, the first thing we did was to spend several hours cleaning before we even began to sit. The kids were surprised. Although good-hearted and idealistic, they paid little attention to their surroundings, but Suzuki Roshi told them, "How can you save the world when you can't even put your shoes straight?"

Sweeping Changes encourages us not to overlook the obvious and close-at-hand possibilities for joy, satisfaction, and fulfillment. With so many calls to consume more goods and travel to picturesque places, we can certainly use more reminders that the beauty of our lives is as close as cleaning a window. Love, kindness, and sincerity come from within and not from yet another object, person, or place. So in Zen, we say, "Let things come and abide in your heart. Let your heart return and abide in things. All through the day and night."

Gary himself is funny in a droll way, quietly absorbing, serious, playful. I haven't seen his house, but if his relationship with me is any indication, it must be companionable.

To be companionable is to touch and be touched, to relate and respond, to be quietly attentive. It is to connect with people and things in a way that reveals and enhances their inherent worth and richness. Let's explore the possibilities of this kind of companionable relationship in our own homes.

Introduction: Zen Practice Comes Home

Many years ago, my parents gave me a suitcase as a high school graduation present. I received other gifts as well, but the suitcase is the one I remember most vividly. When someone hands you a piece of luggage, it can be a less-than-subtle hint that it's time for you to hit the road. But, in this instance, my parents were not trying to propel me directly out the door. Rather, they were setting a process in motion, much as songbirds urge their young to stand, facing outward, upon the high edge of the nest. It was time for me to begin looking at things from a different perspective.

It took me a while to get used to the idea of leaving home. That's understandable when you consider that your home is in many ways an extension of yourself. Whatever sort of place you call home, many of your feelings and attitudes, decisions and life goals are determined there. It's usually the place you get your rest and sustenance, the place where you're most likely to be true to yourself and to have the freedom to dream. It's usually the place where you feel safest, and where you feel less distracted by outside demands and impositions. Whatever your circumstances—whether you are male or female, young or old, living by yourself or with others—your home environment is crucial. Your home outwardly displays many aspects of your personality and aesthetic sense, and often reveals the subtle boundaries between you and the rest of the world. No wonder our homes seem so important to us.

Before leaving home I had, for a couple of years, been working weekends as a musician, and I thought that someday I would earn a living as a jazz pianist. And I did for a few years after setting off on my own. But I almost always had to augment my income by doing other types of work. I was also learning how to keep an apartment, and I had my first real encounters with cooking. A new world was opening itself up to me, giving me both a sense of freedom and a challenging set of responsibilities.

During this period in my life, I became interested in Buddhism and developed a rather rickety, but supportive, Zen practice. Back in the early 1960s, it was hard to find a book (at least in English) on Zen practice, and much of the information that was given to me by friends and fellow musicians turned out to be incorrect and misleading. Still, something about Zen intrigued and fascinated me. Perhaps it had to do with improvisation. As a jazz musician, I found that by throwing myself totally into the creation of the music I was playing, I was experiencing a new kind of clarity, which arrived unannounced, then vanished. This clarity was present at no other time until I began to practice Zen.

The word ZEN has always been an interesting one to me. It's compact, strong, composed entirely of straight lines. It looks like a word turning a corner, and, indeed, that is what many people who study Zen have done. And the corner, itself, then turns and changes as all things do.

Zen is the Japanese word for "meditation," and while this is usually understood as sitting quietly in a formal posture, it can also be applied to the everyday movements of daily activity.

Although most people consider Zen study to be restricted to the confines of monks and hermits and mysterious teachings, this is not always the case. The large majority of people practicing Zen today do so while holding down jobs, going to school, raising families, washing the car, and doing the shopping. As the old teachers said, "Sitting is Zen. Walking, too, is Zen." You study Zen in order to be able to carry your learning and experience into every part of your life. When meditation is integrated into all aspects of your life, it disappears. But your life becomes permanently enriched.

Many people believe that they can't relax and enjoy being at home until the meal is over, the dishes are done, the floor is swept, and other tasks are performed. They assume that drudgery is the price they pay for enjoyment. But that doesn't have to be the case. Indeed, household tasks can be pleasurable and relaxing. There is something soothing about repeating a movement, whether you're sweeping a broom from side to side or using circular motions to dry the dinner plates.

The purpose of practicing Zen is not to experience, in the future, some wonderfully extraordinary event, but to realize that each moment of life is unique and extraordinary, and that each one of us is both quite ordinary and most miraculous. You learn that taking care of all the little details of your life really matters. Having the car serviced is better, both for the car and for you, than neglecting it. Attending to a dripping faucet helps the faucet, the sink, the water source, and yourself. When you give your attention and care to another being or object, your life slowly takes on another shape and begins to have more meaning than before. Your conception of time changes, and your actions become less hurried. And as you become less hurried, you begin to understand yourself a bit better.

Most musicians will tell you that the slow, simple pieces can actually be the most difficult to play. There is less room to cover up your mistakes, and there are fewer opportunities to dazzle the listener by showing off your technique. Each note becomes more resolute and has greater significance. It is in the performance of a romantic ballad, a tender lullaby, or a delicate pavane that the musician's inventiveness, control, and complexity become apparent. In much the same way, the simple tasks of daily life have the potential to tell us the most about ourselves.

Although seated meditation (*zazen* in Japanese) remains the cornerstone of Zen study, we must also attend to all the other details of our lives, such as packing lunches and going to the bank and replacing the soap in the bathroom. Indeed, these everyday tasks, this maintenance of our surroundings—and even daily work for its own sake—are an integral part of Zen practice. In eighth-century China, the master Pai Chang (called Hyakujo in Japan) initiated the use of vigorous everyday work as an element of his teaching. He was not interested in entertaining dreamy-eyed philosophers or those seeking escape from the outside world. The monks who studied with him learned that understanding has its roots in the events of daily life, that action is one of the keys to serenity, and that wisdom resides within the ordinary.

The master teacher Eihei Dogen, who is credited with establishing Soto Zen in thirteenth-century Japan, often quoted an earlier teacher who said, "Working with the sleeves tied back is the activity of way-seeking mind." Dogen showed that by working with something, you can become intimate with its many facets and that this familiarity carries over into all other areas of your life. Along with sitting meditation, he emphasized the importance of how you live your everyday life, including your work, your leisure time, and your personal conduct.

Living at an established place of practice, such as a monastery or Zen center, can be extremely valuable and rewarding, but that's something many people simply cannot or choose not to do. You may live far away from such centers or have other restrictions or responsibilities that do not allow you to attend classes or to meet with other students. Or perhaps you're not interested in immersing yourself in Zen study, but are just looking for a few simple ways to cope with problems or complications in your life. For example, you may be trying to find a bit more meaning or freedom within the confines of raising a family, building a career, or attending school.

Fortunately, studying Zen does not require you to be in a special place. Your own home will do nicely. Zen is everywhere: It is just beneath your feet; it is right in front of your face. You don't have to shave your head or think in exotic ways. There's no need to buy special tools or implements. Zen uses whatever is at hand. It uses not only robes, meditation cushions, incense, and bowing mats, but rags, buckets, brooms, sponges, and sandpaper. It is in the fishbowl and on top of the radio. It is in the action of picking up your shoes and placing them side by side. It's opening a jar or writing a check for the water bill.

Shunryu Suzuki Roshi, founder of the San Francisco Zen Center, told his students, "When you study Buddhism, you should have a general house-cleaning of your mind. You must take everything out of your room and clean it thoroughly. If it is necessary, you may bring everything back in again. You may not want many things, so one-by-one you can bring them back. But if they are not necessary, there is no need to keep them."

The literature of Zen is replete with references to housecleaning. There are stories of priests, monks, nuns, and laypeople dusting, sweeping, shining, polishing, and repairing. They attend to their windows, their doors, their robes, and themselves. They pour water, read letters, and worry about how much rice to cook for dinner. These activities are not somewhere beyond humanity but rather are integral to it. The intricacies and demands of daily life have no end. They are the very framework on which life is woven. And each thread is important in determining the quality of that life.

Have you ever watched children who were engrossed in play or a craft activity, and marveled at their total involvement? We can all learn from them. As the tenth-century Zen master Unmon put it, "When you are walking, walk! When you are sitting, sit! But above all else, don't wobble!"

When you're totally in an activity, you become one with that activity and meet yourself along the way. At times, the activity itself can become positively effortless. In Zen, we speak of throwing ourselves away, or of giving ourselves totally to an action, or of "letting go" of preconceptions. This letting go is what allows the unusual to happen. It might be a perception that transcends anything you have experienced before. Or a brief moment of heightened sensation, when the simple act of opening a cupboard is magnified and given new perspective.

There is much beauty in all that surrounds us, but in order to discover it, we must begin with our feet on the ground, observing in great detail everything that appears before us. There's no doctrine we need to subscribe to, no supplies we need to buy. We already have everything we need in order to make these discoveries. Dogen said, "When you find your place in things, your true practice can begin." For many of us, and for much of the time, this place is inside our own home.

This book examines a variety of everyday activities, putting emphasis on how Zen practice can affect the little daily duties that many people have always disliked: housecleaning chores, meal preparation, and the like. You will be encouraged to relate to your home—its atmosphere, furnishings, and inhabitants—in a different way. I have included some material on Zen's history and about what it means to be a practitioner in today's world. The book's final chapters extend our view of household practice to examine what you can do in your own home or workplace when you don't have access to qualified teachers or a community of fellow students. You will learn about meditation (alone or with friends and family) as well as the rewards of reading. We will explore how conformity, perfectionism, and other subjects relate to day-to-day activity.

Whether you live in an apartment, in a small room, or on a palatial estate, there is plenty of opportunity for learning. My hope is that you will find something of value here. If nothing else, we may all get our houses clean. We may get rid of some unneeded dust. Let's tie back the sleeves of our robes and begin together.

PART ONE

Traveling the Household

This worn-out carpet

   recounts a thousand stories

      as it unravels.

Crossing the Threshold

In ancient times, men and women protected their homes by festooning their doorways with flower garlands, affixing mistletoe or pine boughs to the lintels overhead, or rubbing the doorposts with garlic or other potent herbal mixtures. The custom of a groom carrying his bride across the threshold of their home also has its roots in ancient agriculture. It is believed to have had some connection to "threshing," or using the feet to separate usable seeds and grains from husks and stems, dried straw and chaff. The origins of the word *thresh* are identical to those of *turn, contour, return,* and *thread.* And today, *threshold* not only refers to a doorway or gate, but also means both a new beginning and a limitation.

Throughout the history of Zen, there have been commentaries on gates and doors. Virtually every teacher in every time period has seen the value in directing the student's attention toward these common points of entry. All types of doors—from massive wooden barriers to the famous "gateless" gates—figure in Zen's literature. Students learned early on that doors and gates are not only for walking through but also for thinking about. In fact, in Zen practice, any object or idea can become a door. And behind every door, there is a buddha waiting to be discovered.

Inside your own home, doors do not usually require much maintenance or consideration. A door should have a full range of motion, so keep furniture and other objects a good distance from where the door might strike it. A doorstop will protect both the door and the adjoining wall. You can silence any squeaks with an occasional application of oil. You might, rarely, need to replace worn paint or varnish or to perform a minor adjustment of the hinges or fit. But for all of their continued use, they make few demands on us.

Do not think of doors as obstacles to whatever is on the other side. Practice opening them magnanimously and closing them with care. Through the mundane activity of entering or leaving a doorway, you can make a commitment to being either inside or outside of something larger than yourself. You can think about what you are leaving behind, about what you are entering into. In the Zen training halls, there are rules about opening, closing, entering, and exiting through zendo doors. These rules are liberating. It is one of the great ironies of Zen practice that through the rigid use of such rules, a sense of freedom is gained.

Doors are more than wood or metal, more than hinges, pivots, fulcrums, locks. They are places that can become turning points—either you pass through them, or they block your path. You discover your own limits and thresholds. Sometimes it doesn't take anything very substantial for you to fabricate a closed door. For example, when the lock on a bathroom door is absent or broken, a cough, whistle, or quiet song can bar the door. At other times, it may take a more drastic solution to achieve this effect. The writer Jack London, gregarious as he was, often felt the need for privacy when he was writing. He hand-lettered a small sign for his door to be used at such times: "1. Please do not enter without knocking. 2. Please do not knock."

As you walk from room to room in your own home, try to really experi-

Crossing the Threshold

ence the transition of traveling from one place to another. Notice the differences between motion and stillness. Sense how you relate to various enclosures and open spaces. Feel the differences between entering and leaving, if there *are* differences. Contemplate the thoughts that become caught between places, in the doorways themselves, and think of the people who have walked these paths before you. While you're thinking of others, the doors of your household begin to become the gates of compassion.

Suzuki Roshi stressed repeatedly that, just like the swinging door, we should move freely back and forth throughout the various aspects of our lives, both wholly independent and, at the same time, completely connected to all things. He viewed the very act of breathing as the breath's entering and exiting a doorway. The image of stepping through a doorway is symbolic of your actual entry into your own life. It might be compared to a film loop in which you're entering the same door over and over again. You are always entering through the doorway of this very moment. There is no retreat. No heading for the exits. Just a continual "going in" to this eternal NOW!

The Way of the Broom

Could anything be simpler than sweeping your own floor? Complications arise only when "thinking" interferes with performance. When you become too conscious of your actions, too careful, you can encounter a kind of "nervous" negative energy. Oddly enough, too much thought can result in the same kind of disjuncture as absentmindedness and lack of concentration. When you strain *too* hard to create beautiful music, you fumble the notes and the music suffers. Even sweeping the floor can become awkward and ineffectual if done with too much care.

Fish are not aware that they exist in water, and birds do not "think" about the air. Cows and crickets are, without thinking about it, at ease in their own natural elements. For you to find *your* own natural place, it is helpful to stay in touch with where you are now and what you are doing. Try not to let your thoughts carry you away. Keep bringing yourself back to yourself.

The repetitive motions of sweeping a floor can be a good method for practicing this returning. (Using a high-powered vacuum cleaner may yield more spectacular results, but we're not seeking anything spectacular here.) Try doing some simple sweeping, without noise, without past or future, without premeditation, without stricture, without aim. Just move the broom. Without ambivalence, you can offer your very best. When you sweep in this way, you develop attentiveness rather than mere intention. You watch the broom travel through all the leavings, tracings, tracks, and tiny evidences that show that things are alive all around you. There is dust, there are flakes and crumbs, and there may be mites and spiders. All things are moved along and guided by the traveling broom. Its path determines the path of all that falls before it. Before long, you might lose yourself in the gentle, rocking motion of this easy sweeping.

When you are truly alive, however, you can concentrate wholeheartedly on one task without ignoring the rest of the world. You are still keenly aware of the ticking clock, the telephone, the sound of raindrops on the roof, the smell of baking bread. You see what is before your eyes and hear what is carried to your ears. Relaxing inside yourself, you then allow more things to enter your life. The size of the area being swept in no way limits the extent of your sweeping. And the quality of this sweeping is determined only by your own heart and your own actions. As with everything in life, the act of sweeping can be performed in many different ways. Notice the man standing on the roof of the barn, who sweeps an uneven surface. Or the young child struggling to sweep the kitchen floor with a broom twice her height. Or the smiling shopkeeper who sweeps the cement walkway in front of his store.

There is something so familiar and timeless in this universal act that just thinking about it brings the feeling and memory of the broom handle to your own hands. You can hear the sound of sweeping all around. That sound—made by the movement of the straw over the flat surface of the floor—reminds me of jazz: *Shush, tap! Shush, tap! Shush, tap!* It's like the regular cadence that underlies and defines each song. Things begin to move along on their own. After the sweeping, you hear new sounds: the soft rattle of the dustpan and the thump of the wooden broom handle as it is rested against the wall.

The next time you sweep the floor, try to move with deliberation, feeling both the support of the floor beneath your feet and the protection of the ceiling overhead. Try to sense the differences between rooms, and be aware of changing courses from area to area and from environment to environment. Notice the different qualities of light and the variations of shadows. And experience both the fragility and the strength of your own body as it goes about its common work.

At times in our lives we all experience hunger and headaches, fever and chills, metabolic imbalances, distractions and disorder, near misses, wild diversions, and doubt. Still, we go on sweeping. We do the things that need to be done. We become united with each action. This daily work then becomes a kind of team effort. When we work wholeheartedly, who is not with us? Who is not helping us? Who does not support us in every action and breath?

The uncomplicated act of moving a broom back and forth across a stair step or the kitchen floor can contain all the grace, purpose, and ease of motion that is exhibited in a timeless piece of choreography. The broom is our connection to the ground. It is an extension of our touch. It is the equivalent of the traveling monk's staff, the mountaineer's ice ax, or the shepherd's crook. It helps us to cover and explore the territory. With it, we sweep the dust from our floors, we reach into darkened corners, we retrieve items from under the bed, gather spiderwebs, push open doors, and unclutter our walkways. It is one of the most basic of cleaning implements, the very symbol of simplicity and patience.

Your style of sweeping and the reasons you sweep can reveal much about your personality. Are your strokes generous and open? Or are they short and tightly controlled? Do you use the broom like a broom, or more

The Way of the Broom

like a snow shovel or a canoe paddle? Do you sweep "around things" rather than under them and behind them? Do you give your complete attention to the broom, or are your thoughts drifting and scattering somewhere else? Are you sweeping because you are bothered by the sight of a dusty floor, or because company is coming for dinner and you don't want your guests to find out how messy you really are?

No matter how or why you sweep, you can bring sincerity and art and joy into this singular experience. When you sweep the floor or the stairway or the sidewalk, you can try to make your very best effort. But the point is not to transform the world into an immaculate place; it is to sweep with a sincere heart. With joy, you can perform the little dance steps that occur when you sweep close to your own feet, and you can delight in twisting around to reach the area behind you.

There is a difference between a brand-new broom and an older one. As the broom gets used over and over again, its character is brought forth. If you move the broom from left to right as well as from right to left, the broom will wear more evenly, and, in the process, you'll experience two different sides of yourself. You may notice some awkwardness when you first turn the broom around, just as you feel a bit ill at ease whenever you change your perspective on things. Try to stand a different way or to hold the broom in a different way to see what else happens. Start to give more attention to the floor's edges and corners. Think about your own shadowed areas as well as those that are out in the open.

The broom helps us to stake out our position. It anchors us in the midst of motion. It helps us to orient ourselves in the face of time and space and the subtle teachings of repetitive actions. If we concentrate on just sweeping, the floor and the stairway will take care of themselves. We might even begin to enjoy what once was a tedious chore. Perhaps when we've finished sweeping the floor, we'll practice sweeping shadows or sweeping the moonlight. We might even try sweeping with no broom at all. But this sounds much too heady, and too Zenlike, and our brooms would remain unattended and ignored.

The act of sweeping unites us with our ancestors and with people all over the world. From cave-dwelling times until now, people have gathered bundles of straw and grass in order to sweep clean the flattened surfaces of their lives. And in many parts of the world, dirt floors and walkways are still commonplace. In the hands of the experienced, the broom becomes a multifaceted, functional tool. But no matter how carefully you sweep, you will always find a fine line of dust that still defies the dustpan, or a bit of lint that catches on a loosened splinter of wood. There is always something to remind you of what still needs to be done. There is no way to arrive at "finished." There is no road leading to "perfect." There is just some wandering atom of life, some single bit of dust, that calls you to attention and keeps bringing you back to your life.

The Way of the Broom

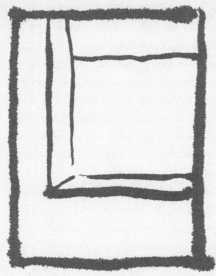

Dusting without Raising More Dust

Where does all of this dust come from, and what does it mean? You leave your home for a few days, and when you return, you are greeted by dust. The Buddha once told his followers that everything they saw before them was only dust. There are histories written in dust. There are entire civilizations buried in dust. Dust is everywhere, and whether it is gold dust, sawdust, or the film that clouds much of our thinking, we must give some kind of attention to it.

Dust is usually defined as fine, dry, particulate matter. It may be composed entirely of soil sediments or of myriad combinations of fine soil and other materials such as wood ash, vehicle exhaust, industrial by-products, pollen, other residual organic matter from both plants and animals, and anything else that can be broken down and suspended in air. In China, certain areas of the earth's surface contain deposits of loess, a dust made of wind-borne sediments, that reach thicknesses of seven hundred feet or more. Geologists estimate that about forty-three million tons of dust settle over the United States each year. Air currents and turbulence are responsible for bringing part of this dust into our own surroundings, and factors such as humidity and ventilation determine its distribution in the home.

Dust figures in one of my favorite stories, about a young Zen monk. Having just moved into a new temple, the monk was filled with energy and dedication and surpassed all the other monks in his zeal for cleaning. During work practice, he was an absolute tornado, running throughout the rooms and hallways, sweeping and polishing and dusting everything in sight. One day his teacher asked him, "What are you doing?" The monk beamed a large smile in the direction of his teacher and said, "I am working hard to clear away the dust of delusion, and to reveal the shining face of Buddha which is beneath it." His teacher said to him, "Please don't ever forget. The dust is also the Buddha."

When it comes to the more mundane household duty of removing the dust from your own shelves, tabletops, furnishings, and possessions, even the word *dusting* becomes suspect. You are actually *de*-dusting or *un*-dusting. Unlike a baker who dusts the breadboard with flour, or a gardener who dusts an area with fertilizer, you are not gaily spreading dust around the perimeters of your home. You're attempting to remove it. But what is really happening here? Is it actually possible to rid your home of dust? How do you dust without raising more dust?

Dusting is an exercise in patience and dexterity. As soon as you begin to dust the things in your life, you are on your way toward learning a lesson in taking things for granted. A bit too much hurriedness or a random distraction, and the vase of flowers is knocked over and broken. A slip of the hand while dusting your desk can scatter your important papers all across the room.

Use the time you dust to enhance your sense of touch. You can experience a feeling of intimacy with the things in your environment by caressing the various objects before you, becoming familiar with their shapes once again, and remembering how they came into your life. As with sweeping, make sure that you give your full attention to those areas that would be easy for you to hurry over or to abandon entirely. The idea is not to go over or around things but to go into them.

It's also important to remember that dust is not vile, unimportant, or without worth. It is, among other things, a living environment for other kinds of beings. Whole universes are contained within just a small amount of this material. Zen students often bow to the dust of the world, in gratitude, just as they would bow to the great mountains, rivers, and forests of the world.

After a productive period of housecleaning, the dust seems to disappear. But this is a delusion; it is merely redistributed. Some of it goes out with the trash or flies with the shaking of the cloth outside, only to be brought back in on the soles of shoes or on wisps of air. Somehow it always manages to find its way back into our lives. It waits for us to find it someplace else. It realizes that it is indispensable. There is a certain beauty to it all. We dust. And the dust finds a way to return. We dust again. In this way, the sweeping and dusting of our lives is never finished. It is much the same as our own breathing, this going out and coming back. It is similar to our recurrent thoughts or feelings, the ones that return to comfort and sustain us throughout the years. Dust, after all, has a certain familiarity and standing in the world. As fragile and transitory as it seems, it offers us a lasting and powerful lesson in how the world is made.

form and Emptiness: Your Space and Possessions

Most children are fascinated with the idea of secrets. You may still remember the thrill you had as a child when you knew something others didn't. Learning to do magic tricks is another way to enjoy secrets. Children take great delight in making things change and disappear, and in amazing an audience with such feats. Later, we all learn ways to envision and change ourselves. We experiment with myth and storytelling, and we develop, slowly, our own sense of what is useful and what is real. I can remember, as a child, lying on the living room floor, looking up at the ceiling, and trying to imagine our house being upside down. I would then be able to walk across the ceiling, and there would be much more room for me to move around. The furniture would all be stuck high overhead, out of the way. And I would have to step up gingerly, over foot-tall transoms, to pass through doorways. It was fun, even then, to invent a new way of doing things and to see the world a bit differently.

But even imagination has its limits. There are always areas and objects in our lives that remain hidden from view. Dogen said that there are mountains hiding everywhere, and that mountains are even "hidden in hiddenness." You will always find that there are things hidden from you throughout your life, but by picking up at least some of the loose ends around you, you begin to locate some of these hidden things. Your life becomes less scattered.

Let's say you're having company for dinner, and you haven't been given much notice. At the last moment, you're scurrying around, straightening up the house, and making things look clean and neat—you are trying to perform a magic act. You're creating an illusion you wish were true. You don't have time to really clean things, so you hit the highlights and concentrate on overall effect rather than wasting time attending to things people won't see. In the context of this particular situation, when your time is limited, all of this rush and distraction are understandable.

But there are many and various places in our home we routinely give too little attention to, such as the bottom drawer of a desk or the top shelf of a closet. There is even a part of ourselves that we would just as soon forget completely. One of my Zen teachers once spoke about "the dog in the basement." This rather wild and uncontrollable creature is the part of our persona that we prefer to keep confined and out of the sight of others. We commit it to some dark corner of our house and hope that it never gets loose. After all, negative things are loud and embarrassing. And we don't know what might happen if this particular dog were to get out into the open, into the bright sunlight.

Part of our sense of order demands that we keep all "wild" things separate. Your yard may have a row of bricks or a wooden edging to distinguish the places you have cultivated from the areas that are weedy, raw, and undeveloped. But life is filled with other lines of demarcation that are invisible and ever changing. Faced with a complexity of decisions, most of us try to keep things under control, but this effort to control our situation can be an unending source of frustration and unhappiness. It seems that some things just won't stay controlled or hidden. Maybe they have their own ideas about the way things should happen.

There is a great relief that comes from learning that we can simultaneously trust in ourselves and in other things. In fact, there is no difference between us and what we think of as "other." When our consciousness resonates with another object, we risk losing control; we open up and we achieve a new kind of compassion. And things begin to control themselves, without our intervention.

The history of the Buddhist term *sangha* illustrates the progression toward an all-inclusive perspective. Originally, it was used to describe those people who were fellow students and practitioners of Buddhism. It often conveyed a feeling of family and of gathering together in Buddhist study. Later, the definition of the word was expanded, by some, to include all sentient beings. Still later in Buddhist development, there were those who argued that the term should include all things, whether they were sentient or not. These people considered stones and sunlight, oceans and teapots, to be part of life's family and deserving of official membership and recognition in the *sangha*. And lastly, there were the real radicals, the ones who asked why there should be any limits or restrictions at all. They insisted that all things should be included in the *sangha, whether they existed or not!*

This may seem ridiculous to you when you first consider it, but does something really need to exist in order for us to take care of it? Don't we prepare the baby's room before the baby arrives? Or keep a loved one's picture even though the person has died? Don't we also care deeply for things that have become lost? Once again, there are ways you can expand your notions and your definitions of limits and boundaries. You can consider the things in your life in a very different way. You can turn the room on its head; you can bring things out into the open and unite with them.

When you're attempting to organize the things within your home, remember that patience and good humor may be your two best friends. Consider what happened to one of my friend's neighbors. This neighbor owned a pet raccoon, which was well cared for and lived in a pen specially built along one wall of the man's rather large apartment. One weekend, the neighbor was called out of town and left the animal alone, with ample food and water to last for several days. After the man had left, the raccoon learned a simple but interesting rule concerning man-made objects: Most things unscrew to the left. The fasteners on the pen opened this way, as did most of the handles and knobs on the drawers and cupboards throughout the apartment. Lightbulbs unscrewed this way. Faucet handles were also turned on in this manner. My friend's neighbor owned an old and expensive, manual typewriter, and the raccoon patiently unscrewed several connecting rods and other machined components and left them on the table. For two days, the busy animal proceeded in this way to quietly dismantle its owner's lodgings, achieving the same effect as a violent explosion in a very quiet and orderly fashion.

The neighbor's household had been carefully maintained and well-ordered. Only one thing had been out of place in his apartment, and that was the raccoon.

Samuel Beckett once said that our job is "to find a form that accommodates the mess." That can be quite a challenge! It's so easy to leave your things scattered in all directions. The day's mail, the half-full glass of fruit juice, the discarded sweater, and the uncapped pen are set down "temporarily." And then something else requires your attention. A few days later, you find yourself wondering: What happened? Where's my pen? And where did all of this *other stuff* come from? How do seemingly inanimate objects migrate from one room to another? Am I living out the chaos theory here in my own life?

Suzuki Roshi said, "Everything should exist in the right place, in the right way. . . . When you do things in the right way, at the right time, everything else will be organized. You are the 'boss.' When the boss is sleeping, everyone is sleeping. When the boss does something right, everyone will do everything right, and at the right time. That is the secret of Buddhism."

Here are a few commonsense rules to follow when you start to put things away in your own home: Position shorter items in front of taller ones. Place lighter things on top of heavier ones. Protect the fragile object from hard, neighboring items that might harm it. Some things always have a tougher time of it than others.

Store each thing carefully, giving attention to the fact that there are differences between caring for something by putting it in a safe place and hoarding it or imprisoning it. Storing items poorly or forgetting about them is no different from abandonment. Even if something is being put away for a great length of time, visit it from time to time, remembering how it came to you, reminding yourself of its value, and checking on its condition. Make periodic inventories of any new possessions you've acquired. Lay them out and look at them. Don't be afraid to acknowledge mistakes you may have made in selecting them. Above all, don't ignore what you have.

When an object is stored away unseen, it faces the dangers of rust and mildew and other deterioration. Buddhist teachers have always counseled their students to keep things simple and in repair, to keep them sharp and shining, and ready to achieve their intended purpose, in a carefully chosen place. Be wary, they say, of the container that is more ornate and complicated than its contents.

Your immediate surroundings are often what best determine the most natural place for an object to rest. The stark beauty of a single stone or flower arrangement or ceramic plate is often enhanced by its location or its isolation. A great pile of flowers or a room filled with teacups detracts from your ability to focus on one of them and to appreciate it. You begin to learn a great deal when you can bring your careful attention to one single object. Many of the works of poets, such as Pablo Neruda, are the result of such careful observation; these odes cast the most common of household objects—the scissors, the spoon, the onion, or the loose and wayward thread—in an entirely new light.

A scanning electron microscope can reveal a forest of bristles at the end of your toothbrush, the cratered moonscape of the pencil's point. There is no end to what we can learn through careful observation. But observation also should be extended into the open spaces of our lives. Modern particle physics and various theories of quantum mechanics regarding dynamic variables have confirmed many Buddhist ideas about emptiness. It exists (or doesn't exist) in all molecules, atoms, and structural particles. Things are linked by emptiness as well as structure. There is no form without emptiness, no emptiness without form. Yet we do not live in empty space. We live here in this everyday world, in this time, and in this household. We must deal with things like wildness and randomness, and with the abandoned, hidden, and misplaced.

The classic Japanese artists who brought the woodcut to worldwide attention often began their work by printing the pure blackness of a "perfect" board. Only after doing this did they begin to carve away the surface of the wood, which interfered with its "true spirit," and to create their works of art. (This is another way of emptying one's house and of utilizing only what is needed.)

It is said that everything has its place, but many of us simply have too many things. The more things you have, the less time you have to spend with each one individually. You find one thing lost behind another, one obscuring or completely covering another, and other things missing altogether. Things lose their usefulness and become obstacles. You step on the misplaced shoe or trip over the tossed pillow. At such times, don't focus on wanting to be forever, fanatically tidy; instead, remind yourself not to be "unfair to your surroundings," to use Suzuki Roshi's phrase.

The spirit of your home is very important. It might be filled with all the various items that bring some joy to your life, or it might be more austere. Whatever the case, it should simply reflect who you are. But when you have the feeling that you're being crowded out of your own surroundings, that your spirit is being lost and overwhelmed by your own possessions, then it's time to begin gathering the tossed, the neglected, and the forgotten elements of your home and to look at them realistically.

Clear out those possessions you no longer need or want: Whisk your old books off to the library. Give clothing to those who need it more than you do. And if you have two of *anything,* give away at least one of these items. Many of us hold back something, some object, thinking that someday we might need it. If you don't use it, get rid of it, make it disappear. This project is a lot like weeding the garden, for it gives the things that live with you enough room to flourish.

There are many who would have better lives if only we would pass along to them those things that sit unused or duplicated among our own possessions. The "yellow pages" section of the phone directory has many listings of charitable organizations, both local and international, which can distribute your contributions. Giving things away in this manner has ongoing benefit for everyone. What do you have to lose?

Dogen told his students that there was no need for them to ever own anything that had to be hidden from others. Before you bring new things into your life, ask yourself where you'll keep them, how they will be maintained, and what amounts of precious time will be traded in order to gain their purchase. Think more in terms of letting things go rather than in acquiring, clutching, or owning. As Ralph Waldo Emerson said long ago, "Things are in the saddle and ride mankind."

Determine whether you acquire things because of fad, fashion, or the timeless quest for acceptance by others. If all of this advertising and designer-labeling of things really increases their value, why do so many of these items end up in the sale bins, mark-down racks, and remainder outlets? Even there, we are urged to snap them up, whether we need them or not, because they are a "bargain." There is no need for us to sacrifice having things we truly need, but it's important to consider our actions. Try not to be blinded by the advertising slogans. And don't be misled by impulse or fantasy.

There is a story of a Zen monk, centuries ago, who fell into delusion and decided that he wanted nothing other than to possess the moon. One night while out on a walk, he found the moon in a puddle of clear rainwater. He carefully scooped it out, put it into a bottle, and took it back to his room. Sitting at his small desk, he poured the water out, into another container. But the moon was gone.

Sometimes it seems as though marketing people are always promising us the moon. Product advertising and salesmanship are ubiquitous, invasive, and, worst of all, tempting. We are constantly being shown how happy we will be once we have brought chosen items into our lives.

Zen teachers, beginning with Joshu (eighth–ninth centuries) have cautioned that happiness is not a matter to be decided by picking and choosing. It is much more important that we learn how to "discern." What *is* this thing? What does it do? Does it have value, use, or purpose for me? Where does it come from? What plants or animals were sacrificed or exploited in its manufacture? Can I get along without it? Is there someone else who has a greater need for it?

People visiting developed nations from less privileged countries spend hours, if not days, in our stores and markets just looking at the vast aisles of merchandise on display. There are overwhelming numbers of choices to be made. To newcomers, our stores are like museums. Even neighborhood corner shops are filled with merchandise of every sort.

The contemporary Vietnamese Zen teacher Thich Nhat Hanh once took a group of young children to a large hardware store in France, where they live. Before they entered the store, he informed them that the only thing they would be buying was a supply of nails for some repair work he had in mind. However, he told them they could spend as much time looking at things as they wanted. So the Zen master and the children spent several hours going from shelf to shelf, item to item, looking at everything in the store. After they had finished, they all walked to the cashier, purchased the nails, and left. The wonderful thing about this story, for me, is not that they exhibited some stoic sense of willpower, but that they entered already knowing the outcome and still took time to confront the wide array of things, looking directly at all that called to them, and learning about what was there.

If your storage space is limited, try using shelves and tables designed expressly for corners. Storage containers for under the bed and other out-of-the-way places can also help. If this isn't possible, take every opportunity to practice your own brand of magic. Make small baskets disappear inside large baskets; put tiny items inside slightly larger ones.

Sometimes your surroundings may seem to be a bewildering swirl of motion, a ruckus of gadgets, memories, thoughts, and treasures. Centuries ago, the priest Kyozan asked Master Isan, "When a hundred thousand things come at me all at once, what should I do?" Isan replied, "Blue things are blue, yellow things are yellow. These things have no interest in helping or harming you. Don't worry about them. All things have their own place in the Universe."

When you put your summer clothes away, you are putting a real summer into the storage chest. When you add a new jar of spice to the kitchen cupboard, you are putting a special harvest away for future use. As you put each thing into its place, look beyond the hindrances of ownership and possession and realize the value of all things. You will then begin to experience an unbounded space.

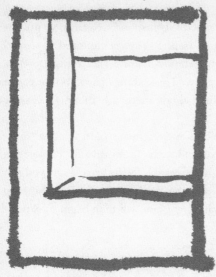

A World of Windows

Windows are doorways of light. The more windows you have in your life, the more illumination there is, and the more chances you have of seeing what's around you. When you begin looking *at* windows, rather than through them, you can also discover things that might otherwise be lost. A window is both a transparent opening and an invisible boundary. It helps to separate what is inside from what is outside. It defines some unseen division of territory, a line of clarity that straddles the visible and the faraway world, and becomes both an enclosing barrier and a new, beginning point of vision.

Interestingly, when shadows and lighting conditions change and come together in different ways, the window becomes a mirror. Not only does the glass now become visible, but we become visible to ourselves. The reflecting surface of glass partially obscures the differences between "inside" and "outside," as images indoors are superimposed over those beyond our walls, making them appear more unified. This new way of seeing things can be a hidden virtue of glass that is not too transparent, not too clean.

Taking care of your windows can be a richly rewarding experience, especially if you clean your windows on a sunny day. You can feel the warmth of the sunlight radiating toward you from far away. As you attend to this cleaning, you might wonder about what you're seeing. What do you look for when you seek more clarity in your life? What is it that interferes with experiencing this clarity? How far does clarity extend? And while cleaning windows primarily engages your sense of sight, there are sounds to experience as well. Listen to the sounds of the squeaking as your cloth wipes the glass, and the sound of dripping water as you wring out the washing cloth. The poet Santoka said, "In the never-ending sound of water, you will always find the Buddha."

When Zen students wash their windows, they try to avoid leaving water marks or streaks behind. They try to enter every action fully without leaving any traces in their activity. By the same token, they try not to create any unneeded shadows in their thinking and to find freedom and joy in each experience. Careful practice may help you to discover a sense of "mind, as clear as glass." And by concentrating on the simple wiping motion of the washcloth, you may begin to feel the origins of your own emancipation.

It is important, however, not to become "fixated." There is no need for you to be relentless. It is more a matter of finding the easiness that comes from using your own quiet energy. There's no need to strive for total cleanliness and purity. Even perfect clarity is not without its problems. A perfectly transparent window is a danger to flying birds and insects. And water that is perfectly clear is not a healthy environment for fish; it leaves them no place to rest or to hide from their pursuers. A window is clean enough when it can naturally serve its purpose. By cleaning each window regularly, with care and confidence, you will allow your home to be filled with more of spring, more of winter.

When you allow more light into your life, you are better equipped to see things as they are, to more objectively appreciate the beauty and importance of your life. Dogen described this kind of objectivity as being able to look at flowers without demanding more color, or being able to observe the moon without asking it to have more brightness. As you allow yourself to open more fully to your experience, you gain a connectedness to things. You can enjoy the light of the sun, moon, and stars, and also the sound of the curious puppy rubbing her nose against the windowpane.

As you finish washing one window, you are already moving on to the next one, brightening the interior of your living space, and bringing the world outside into clearer focus. Again, this simple task becomes a way of gathering things together.

The Idea of Maintenance

Maintaining your home is demanding work. The fact that certain things must be done regularly, day in and day out, almost guarantees that you will approach them in a desultory and spiritless manner. You do housework as a matter of cleanliness, but you're also trying to preserve and protect your home and furnishings. However, Buddhism teaches us that maintaining any consistent state of things is not possible: Everything will change, deteriorate, and disappear eventually. All things are nonabiding. Everything you see might as well be stamped "temporary" and "ephemeral."

No matter how carefully you treat the things you live with, there will come a day when the cupboard door will loosen and fall from its hinges, and when the chair you're sitting in will start to give way. Your life and all that's in it are simply on loan to you and are clearly precarious. Even your breath is fleeting, and every beat of your heart is transitory.

For me, the most exciting art forms have always been the "fugitive" ones, those that use real time as their arena, such as theater and live music. Anything can happen during a performance. Things may go amiss, or it can be one of those transcendental experiences. When you're caught up in a spellbinding action on stage, or totally immersed in a clarinet sonata or jazz improvisation, you aren't thinking about how everything will end. You don't question the goal or the reason or the process of the work. You are *involved* at once with the actors or the musicians. There is nothing else, other than this beautiful moment that surrounds you. You are *moved* emotionally, with no thought of stopping time in order to preserve the experience.

In much the same way, Zen teachers have shown that we can make each instant of our lives vital and important. It is impossible to remove one single lightning flash of time, no matter how boring or unimportant it may seem, without annihilating all sense of present, past, and future. In fact, all time exists in this very moment. When you bring energy and attention into each of your activities, you are no longer engaged merely in maintenance. You're still involved in taking care of things, but you bring this caring into an immediate and more creative plane. As you straighten up the medicine cabinet, you just roll back your sleeves and do your best. Sometimes when working in this way, intently and intimately in contact with some small task, you may start to sense the connectedness in things.

Indeed, all things on Earth are interconnected. Since the days of ancient Greece, there have been stories of Gaia, the earth mother and goddess of the world. Her name has been applied to the more recent scientific theories that regard Earth as a self-contained, complete, organic entity. Earth's rivers, creeks, and oceans function as a circulatory system, and its atmosphere is a kind of skin. Scientists are quick to point out that the health of the planet depends on forests, streams, microclimates, and clouds working together in balance. No small part of the earth is insignificant. There is nothing in nature that doesn't have purpose.

It might be interesting to look at your own home as an organic unit. The outer skin (the walls) contains water, heating, and air circulation systems. Inside, your basic living space can be altered by what you bring into it, in much the same way food acts upon your own body. Just as weather is determined by different pressure systems coming into contact with one another, the feelings generated in your home living space are determined by the things you place around you: the kind of music you listen to, the food you prepare, the relationships you foster, the books you read, and the dozens of other everyday choices you make. No small part of your home is isolated or insignificant. To have a healthy home, you need to have door hinges that don't squeak and a ceiling that doesn't leak when it's raining. You do what's required to help all things work as they were designed to work.

Some people go to such lengths to protect the items in their homes that they can't enjoy their surroundings. I once went with a friend to visit his parents, who lived in a very expensive six-room apartment on San Francisco's Nob Hill. All the furniture and decorative objects were expensive items of fine design. And every single thing in their home was covered in clear plastic! The lamp shades were in plastic bags, the couches and chairs had transparent vinyl coverings, and long plastic runners protected the floors and carpets. I naively asked if they were painting the apartment. And my friend's mother seemed both impatient and offended as she told me that they were not, indeed, painting, and that this was the way things always were. I could hardly believe they lived this way. They sat and walked and ate on plastic and uncovered their beautiful possessions only when they held dinner parties every two months or so. The mother asked us if we might like to try one of the delicious oranges they had just brought from the market. My friend, her son, nodded his head. Then she asked him if he would mind eating it outside. So out the back door he went. The goddess Gaia must have been scratching her head that afternoon.

Please don't be compulsive about your home. You don't need to go through your house, armed with rags and scrapers, seeking out the enemy. Nor do you need to coat your life in protective plastic or antibacterial sprays. When you act out of compulsion, you lose the best of your intentions and weaken your own living experiences. It's fine to rinse and dry the kitchen sink, but don't fret over every pit and stain in the sink's surface. There is a Buddhist saying, "When we seek the Buddha in the mountaintops, we ignore the Buddha in the valley." In other words, when you become overly concerned with purity, self-image, and control, you run the risk of interfering with your own sense of well-being. You ignore your ability to relax and enjoy your own place of residence, and there will always be something sideways in your life.

The place where you live should reflect your true attitude, your true nature. Each room of your home, even a temporary motel room for that matter, can be imbued with personality. You can change or adjust the lighting, add flowers, arrange new elements, and improve conditions, in much the same way as the changing conditions of Gaia affect the climate and mood of the planet. By being in harmony with your surroundings, you will grow more comfortable with who you really are. Whether you're walking along the naturally occurring edge of a creek bed or the shining aisles of a supermarket, you can have a sense of unhurried order and trust in things.

Maintaining your home requires diligence. You develop the habit of continually caring for something you know will change. In spite of our bravest thoughts and actions, everything in our lives remains temporary. The joy comes not from trying to keep things forever, but from keeping them well.

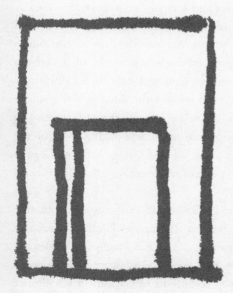

On Changing Colors

It has been nearly a month now since I fell off my ladder or, more correctly, fell *with* my ladder. I was painting an outside wall of our house and was about eight feet from the ground, with a freshly opened gallon can of paint in one hand and a brush in the other, when the ladder collapsed. There was not quite enough time for my life story to pass before my eyes. After the hard and sudden impact, I stood upon, and crouched over, the flattened ladder—

feeling like a demented surfer riding a freak wave. (This kind of thinking is one of the drawbacks of growing up in California.)

A high arc of paint had traveled across the wall like a comet, so I quickly limped over to get the garden hose and then soaked the wall with water, washing the paint away before it had a chance to dry. Aside from a few lacerations and some memorable bruises on my knees and shins, no major damage was done. I didn't break any bones or hit a window.

People say that preparation is half the work of painting. But you don't always know what to prepare for. You think you've got it all figured out when something comes along to give you a slap and wake you from your complacency. *This . . . is the way it is,* it says. *Don't take it personally because it's not about you; it's about This.*

Each step in painting a wall, each stroke of the brush, has the potential to be either trivial or spectacular. Dogen compared the entire universe to the act of painting. Painting is one way in which you can effect obvious change. Sometimes, plain old washing and scrubbing just doesn't do enough to enliven a room or the outside of your house. You may need to resort to a more decisive measure and bring some different colors into your life. For many of us, this can be a joyful, positive, and rewarding experience. For others, it is something to be done only when all else in one's life has failed.

In a way, painting is one of the most elementary of activities. Here, you have something to be painted. There, is your paint and brush. Go! It is the perfect time to practice what is known as nonthinking. Not "not-thinking." *Non*thinking. You just go right ahead and paint. If you think too much about it, you will probably make a mistake. You will become fussy, nervous, and overly cautious, and will probably end up dropping your brush. And if you don't think at all about what you're doing, who knows what kind of mess you'll make? The idea is to just keep painting, fully aware of what you're doing but not *thinking* about it. Let your arms and fingers, your legs and your paintbrush do the work.

You may wonder why, if Zen Buddhists embrace the universe and all its colors, there is so much "blackness" in it (the black cushions, black robes, etc.). This blackness is the blackness of practicality and tradition. In Japan, black and dark indigo were the dyes that were both plentiful and inexpensive. These colors also were very practical because they didn't show dirt and wear. In other parts of the world, Buddhists may wear robes of other colors. I like to think of "Zen black" as the blackness that contains all other colors. Katagiri Roshi said, "If you do a painting of a pine tree, and use only blank ink, that one color will create many colors."

Painting is a material way of protecting something from the elements and of bringing change and color into your life. It's also a wonderful way to observe how changes can occur. In much the same way that mixing blue with yellow will produce green, a blending of your actions and your awareness can lead you to something new and previously unseen.

Enjoy the many subtleties of color in your life, and take pleasure in adding new ones from time to time. To paint is to affirm your trust in things—but never take your eyes off your ladder.

On Style: The Things with Which You Live

When you are deciding what furnishings to bring into your home, you might consult a home decorating magazine or an interior decorator. Before you do, take a moment to ponder the difference between fashion and style. For me, those things that are in fashion are found at the very top of a trend or tendency and are much touted and heavily advertised. They are quite likely to be the topic of conversation and media attention. But style is something else again. There seems to be almost no rule for it. It is a flower that blossoms in many surprising ways. When you see an example of true style, you recognize it immediately. It's not something you acquire by mimicking others or by keeping up with the latest fashion trends.

I learned an important lesson about style while playing in a basketball game in the seventh grade. We were the hosts that afternoon to a team from another school, a school whose student body consisted mainly of the children of agricultural workers. Their school, today, would be referred to as "financially impaired." While we had been outfitted in colorful shorts and silky, embroidered tank tops, the other team's players wore Levi's and plain, white T-shirts. But each player on their team had taken long strands of ribbon, in their school's bright colors, and had tied them to the belt loops of their jeans. And even though we won the game that day (we were a much larger school with a greater roster of athletes), the other team had a spirit that left us stunned. They worked, fought, yelled encouragement constantly to each other, and ran without rest up and down the court with their ribbons flying. We had won the game, but we were aware that in some other ways, they were the better team. A few days later, some of us tried to recapture some of the spirit we had seen by tucking a few ribbons into the tops of our shorts and yelling inspiring messages to our fellow teammates, but it wasn't the same. We had all experienced our first brush with style. It had nothing to do with winning or with what was fashionable. It had to do with unreserved spirit.

The American Zen teacher Maurine Stuart learned a valuable lesson in style when she first met her teacher, Soen Roshi. The two sat quietly for some time in meditation. Afterward, as he informed her that he would agree to be her teacher, he mentioned to her that he was very impressed with her style. When Maurine objected and offered her opinion that style was superficial and should not be considered nearly as important as sincerity, effort, and good intention, Soen said, "No, no, no, style is *very* important."

People who come to Zen centers for the first time are often initially impressed by their ambience. They enjoy the quiet and serenity there, which is facilitated by the absence of the usual clutter found in most of our homes. Most Zen centers are places of at least some degree of communal living, and keeping things simple is a practical step toward the resident's own self-preservation. Some visitors hope to carry this peaceful feeling home with them, and attempt to decorate their own residences in a rather stark, Japanese style. They furnish their rooms with futons, bamboo mats, paper lamp shades, and the like. If you are interested in Japanese architecture and culture and would like your home to resemble a zendo, there is certainly nothing wrong with this. However, it might be good for you to ask yourself, sincerely, whether this might be an affectation.

There are a great many ways to achieve a feeling of peacefulness in your surroundings. You might try using natural and complementary materials (such as water and stone) in different ways, gently curving and unbroken lines, colored or softer lighting, or an arrangement of favorite plants. This doesn't have to be done in a way that emulates a Zen center. It can all be of your own choosing. There is no right or wrong when it comes to arranging your own home, but you will be happier if you make decisions that come from your own heart.

When choosing furnishings, give yourself plenty of time. Don't mistake being impulsive for daring or courageous decision making. Impulsiveness is wonderful when you're looking for a new flavor of ice cream, but with furniture, you have to live with your selection for a very long time. Try to choose items that have some kind of relationship to whatever else is already in the room. (If you're starting with an empty room, be very careful about selecting the first piece of furniture that you bring into it.) Respect the space around each piece. Give your furniture room to breathe.

For some reason, most of us have a different way of presenting our homes to others than we do to ourselves. When company has been invited, we clean and polish, and arrange bowls of flowers. We open windows to let in some fresh air. And we're less likely to leave our underwear hanging from the lamp shade or a half-eaten apple sitting by the phone. Often, by ourselves, we give less attention and consideration to those rooms or areas of our home that visitors seldom see. We have a different standard for ourselves. We are like a business that keeps two different sets of books: one for our eyes only and the other for visitors to review. In Japanese, there are words for these differences: *omote,* what's in front, or the surface of things; and *ura,* what's in back, the reverse. Studying Zen is only one way in which we can try to integrate these two sides of our nature, to fold up the screens and open the doors, and live out in the open as we really are.

When you go on a camping trip or begin to pack for a vacation, you learn to carry with you only those things that are really necessary. You try to avoid the frivolous, the weighty, the insignificant, and the redundant. You try to take only those things you need to take, and no more. At home, you have more room to stretch out, to add a few extras, to bring in objects that give you pleasure. Many people are drawn toward art, antiques, or other collectibles. But a high percentage of them are making their purchases for the wrong reasons. They acquire a painting or a book collection not because they like it but because they believe that someone they are trying to impress will like it. They seek some kind of stature or acceptance or hope they'll be perceived as knowledgeable or having "taste." And, ignoring the real feelings inside themselves, they devote much time and spend a great deal of money searching for that which is illusory, *omote,* the outward surface of the thing.

But it is wonderful when you find something in your life you truly enjoy. A work of art can enhance a room as well as bring joy to your daily life. It can, and should, have its own personality and spirit of life. It can be both a focal point and a complement to the things around it. You can exercise as much care in the selection of your kitchen utensils as you would when purchasing an expensive piece of sculpture. In many parts of the world, throughout time, people have integrated the art of self-expression into the crafting of everyday objects: lovely combs, spoons, teapots, and wearing apparel. Mass-market manufacturing has taken the art out of everyday objects, but you can still look for items that are made with care. Avoid the things you don't need, but when you do buy something, respect it as you would something you had made yourself.

When you have finished acquiring, decorating, and arranging, you can step back and see what you've brought upon yourself. Your home now has a certain style and spirit. The question is: Will you find yourself living on a dinner plate or in the soup? Either way, your home will be an extension of yourself, subject to a wide variety of conditions, needful of caring maintenance, capable of growth, and quite susceptible to change. As the Zen teachers are so very fond of telling us, nothing is forever. This most certainly relates to home decor.

The 10,000 Things That Hide within Plain Sight

Everything around us is interesting—if we take the time to look closely. Let's start with the lightbulb. This everyday item has its own special poetry and delightful qualities: the delicacy of its touch, the fine strength of its filaments, the pear-shaped glass that holds the glow, its literal and figurative "lightness," and so forth. Each lightbulb is a truly wonderful thing, performing its task in the world and fulfilling our wish to bring light into the darkness. We can also consider the invention of the lightbulb; the manufacture, shipping, and marketing of lightbulbs; and their worth, purpose, care, and replacement.

If you had to make your own lightbulbs, how would you do it? By considering such a question, you realize the complexity of these "mundane" objects. What about pencils and toothpaste tubes and toasters? What if you had to make these things yourself? What would you do then? Would you lead a simpler life?

It seems to me that the least we can do, after taking a close look at the many things we've brought into our homes, is to show them our gratitude, much as we might thank our friends. So when you exchange the batteries in your flashlight, take a moment before throwing out the old ones to consider what they have brought to you, the things they have illuminated, the accidents they have prevented, and the items they have helped you find. You can give them one moment of respect, one moment of thanks, one moment of thought.

If you're like most people, you probably have a fairly large amount of "stuff" stored in your home, and a lot of it is rather small and innocuous: candles, pot holders, scissors, clocks, smoke detectors, telephones, and other handy merchandise that helps you run your household. Much of this collection is likely taken for granted, and it is only when something becomes inoperative that you give it any attention at all. Yet these things constitute a kind of support group for you. They offer you safety, convenience, and mobility in a multitude of ways, and many provide other kinds of solace as well.

Each thing in your home—indeed each thing in this world—exists, due to cause and effects, in its own natural way. The candle exists because of darkness. The blanket exists because of the cold. And the spider exists because of the long line of spiders that existed and replicated before it. When left alone, things naturally return to their own wild state. When you leave the woodshed unattended and uncared for, the termites arrive in great numbers, the mice become more assertive, and weeds thrive between the cracks in the floorboards. Each thing finds its perfect opportunity for existence and arrives right on schedule. Wildness has its own wisdom, and there is no denying its resilience and determination.

We have considered where the objects in our lives come from and how we can organize them. But how do we account for our sense of order? Why do we arrange the silverware in its little drawer just so? Why are designers so attracted to straight lines and square corners? And why does the chaos of the back closet contradict all visible evidence of neatness and order elsewhere in the house?

Usually the larger pieces of furniture and the major appliances remain, more or less, in place. It is the smaller items that seem to need arranging and proper placement. We try to bring order to our lives this way. We align the doormat to the wall, categorize cookware, straighten pictures and lamp shades, organize clothing, and become truly infatuated with the symmetrical, the straight, the flat and unwrinkled, and the well-behaved. The danger here is that we might also begin to lose track of the way things really are, of how and why these things exist, and of how easy it is to encourage an unreasonable sense of orderliness in ourselves. If you were to polish one area of the floor compulsively, you would wear the wood away. And when you become obsessed with knife sharpening, you grind away the blades of your knives before their time. They have become so sharp, in fact, that they have disappeared. The objective is to find a balance somewhere between the wildness of the woodshed and the impractical sterility of the home as chemical laboratory, to find a place where there is both cleanliness and comfort, order and surprise. The small things around us seem to find their own places then, places of appropriateness that are free of artifice and interference. And things seem to fall together naturally, bringing a new warmth and harmony to our homes.

In this way, we begin to have a relationship with things. The objects around us become part of our lives rather than just being consigned to the areas of the misused, the fragmented, and the forgotten. There is a kind of wisdom that reveals itself to us when we do the simple actions called for in maintaining the tiny, simple merchandise of the home. We discover the hidden intimacy of things by running a lightly dampened cloth over the telephone, rubbing a bit of lemon oil into the tabletop, airing out the books and blankets, stacking the pot holders near the stove, removing the crumbs from the toaster, and changing the water in a vase of flowers. Things begin to quiet down. We conserve energy and learn the value of silence and darkness. We begin to trust things because we know them better, and we begin to realize a place where there are things beyond value. It all just keeps getting more and more interesting.

On Things Becoming Lost, Broken, or Worn

There is simply no end to the shifting images that parade before us. If you began making a list of all the people and objects that you've encountered in your life, it would take a near eternity. Just try to remember the number of things that have already passed through your hands. And imagine those in the future that have not yet been revealed to you. People and things make their way into our lives constantly, and then depart again.

When you spill the milk, drop the glass bowl, or put the broom handle through the lamp shade, you may become mad at yourself and think: *How could I do such a thing? How could I be so careless? What a mess!* You wish you could rewind your action, correct it, and replay it. Consider, though, that these accidents, these unstudied and spontaneous moments, help you to better appreciate the things that have spilled or been broken. Such moments also show you that you can still be surprised. You feel a surge of adrenaline. You feel invigorated and strange and powerless. You feel, at least for the moment, more charged, more aware and alive.

Buddhism is quick to point out that nothing we see or experience is permanent or unaffected by the transitory nature of existence. In fact, this may be considered to be Buddhism's first law. It is the one true thing that can be depended upon: that all things are unreliable and temporary. This is not exactly what most people care to hear. The haiku poets developed this transitory aspect of existence into a high art form. In the most abbreviated of poetic forms, an arrangement of just seventeen syllables in three written lines, these poets sought to convey the essence of one brief moment of their own lives and to freeze this moment forever, making it always available to us.

Dogen wrote, "All things are Buddha. . . . To carry yourself forward in order to experience things is your delusion. But to allow things to come forward on their own and to experience themselves is enlightenment." How can you give all things the freedom to experience their own natures? Simply by looking at things as they are, and not interjecting your own values, personality, preferences, or judgments upon them. So when you wipe up the milk that spilled and sweep up the shards of broken glass, try to focus on the fact that some things will not last forever, and that there can be an element of danger or surprise in even the most benign occasion. You can then begin to confront the many possibilities inherent in all endings and beginnings.

Although it's said that we live in a "disposable" society, we recognize that some of the things in our lives are irreplaceable: cherished photographs, gifts we've received, certain works of art, and so on. Buddhism shows that, in fact, nothing is replaceable. Each thing before us is precious

On Things Becoming Lost, Broken, or Worn

and unique; it has its own nature and spirit. And each thing will disappear in its own time and way. Remember "to allow things . . . to experience themselves." Don't just ignore or try to discard the little unpleastantries and mistakes that you don't want to deal with. There are many intractable things in life that are not that easily gotten rid of. And there is a world of difference between your letting go of something and your trying to throw it away.

When you break something, is your first impulse to throw it away? Or do you repair it but feel a twinge of sadness because it is no longer "perfect"? Whatever the case, you might want to consider the way the Japanese treated the items used in their tea ceremony. Even though they were made from the simplest of materials, clay and basic glazes, these teacups and bowls were revered for their plain lines and spiritual qualities. They were treated with the utmost care, integrity, and respect. For this reason, a cup from the tea ceremony was almost never broken. When an accident did occur and a cup was broken, there were certain instances in which the cup was repaired with gold. Rather than trying to restore it in a way that would cover up the fact that it had been broken, the cracks were celebrated in a bold and spirited way. The thin paths of shining gold completely encircled the ceramic cup, announcing to the world that the cup was broken and repaired and vulnerable to change. And in this way, its value was even further enhanced.

People tend to cover up their mistakes, to restore things to how they were before, to pretend that everything has been fixed and that things are the same as they were before and that their hearts have not been broken. In actuality, things do break. They do melt. They do let you down occasionally. And in the course of time, *you* also break and change; you become "strong in the broken places," as a country song puts it. You try to learn from your experiences and to share, rather than hide your humanity.

We can all appreciate new things because we sense a freshness about them, a vigor and potential lacking in something old and worn. Yet it is through age and use that objects, as well as living beings, develop character. There is something satisfying about the smooth feeling of a much-used tool, an old and comfortable sweater, a familiar and often-read book. We can learn to appreciate the ancient and scarred oak; to look at all the lines and seams and chipped surfaces of things and see their service and their true beauty; to value that things "are as they are."

During times of great misfortune, when a loved one dies or a house is consumed by fire, people will tend to pause and look for meaning in what's happened. But even life's tiny everyday occurrences—the sparrow hopping along the front porch, the spreading puddle of milk on the floor, the worn cutting board—offer you a chance to contemplate and learn something about your life. In fact, these moments demand that you give genuine attention to them. They are calling out for you to share yourself with them totally because only in this way will they fully exist for you.

Shrines, Altars, and Icons: Places of Homage in Your Home

One blustery December afternoon, I was invited to the apartment of some friends whose home I had not visited before. After warm greetings at the door, I stepped into their living room and almost collided with a massive, Steinway grand piano. There it stood, nearly filling the room, black and glistening and as powerful and out of place as a racehorse. After skirting gingerly around the side of this imposing instrument, we found a sofa and chairs against a far wall and sat down to have tea and share a pleasant conversation. It was only after twenty or thirty minutes had elapsed that I dared to ask about the piano. I had no idea that either of my friends had a talent for music, and I was genuinely interested in knowing who played. My question seemed to embarrass them both a bit; as it turned out, neither of them had ever touched the piano's keyboard. The sole purpose of the piano was to serve as an elegant pedestal on which to display a host of silver-framed family photographs.

To use a piano this way, as a kind of seventy-thousand-dollar end table, may be wildly extravagant, but the significance of my friends positioning their family's images in this fashion should not be overlooked. Most of us have, somewhere in our homes, a place where special items are kept, a place reserved for things most dear to our hearts or set aside for special consideration. It might be a fireplace mantel displaying trophies, a wall lined with family portraits, or a shrine to nature or to loved ones. And it doesn't necessarily have to be within the home. It could be a wallet that sequesters a photograph or lock of hair, or even the car's rearview mirror, which holds a small polished stone on a chain. Regardless of whether this place is imbued with a feeling of heightened respect or spirituality, it has been given a special significance.

Buddhists put a wide variety of shrines and altars in their temples and practice centers. These range from the most elaborate and ostentatious of productions to others as simple as a blade of grass. There are golden statues of the Buddha that were so large and expensive to produce that they nearly bankrupted the countries in which they were manufactured. And there are the lighthearted altars and shrines of students where one can find the Buddhist deities sitting next to Mickey Mouse or Gumby, exhibiting an honest mixture of the seriously religious with the more mundane and capricious aspects of people's lives. I should point out to those unfamiliar with Buddhism that paying homage to any of these shrines or sculpted figures in no way constitutes the worshiping of idols. Practitioners of Zen, in particular, are quite aware that these objects are merely a particular arrangement of metal, wood, stone, or plastic. Yet, like a photograph, they remind us of something that we hold particularly dear. They are an extension of the very qualities that we would like to develop within ourselves. When we bow to them or stand silently for a moment before them, we offer the same respect and acknowledgment that we might give to a long-lost friend. We recognize something outside of ourselves that is still a part of us.

For five hundred years following Buddha's death, his likeness was por-

Shrines, Altars, and Icons

trayed only symbolically, by the image of a footprint, the Bodhi tree under which he sat in meditation, or by a rendering of the sacred wheel. Today, there are Buddhist temples filled with all kinds of rich and inspiring images: various manifestations of the Buddha himself, a host of bodhisattvas (a bodhisattva is an enlightening being who teaches and helps others) such as Jizo and Senju Kannon (the Kannon of a thousand arms). There are unchu kuyo bosatsu (bodhisattvas on clouds) and hibutsu (hidden buddhas, kept behind doors, etc.) and a large collection of gods and guardian figures for all occasions: Fijin (wind god), Raijin (thunder god), Katoku Seikun (fire god), and Fudo Myoo (the supreme deity of the Estoeric doctrines who has brought his raging form to Earth vowing to teach all sentient beings who are stubborn and unteachable). Each one of these figures has its own unique history, purpose, and emphatic qualities, and the mythologies surrounding them have always been an important part of Buddhism. Zen temples have taken this panoply of paintings and sculpture and pared it down to fit into the lean and clean lines for which Zen is famous. The Zen meditation halls often contain only one or two images as focal points, their theme being "nothing extra."

If you choose to set aside a special area in your own home for homage or reflection, a place that is comfortable and out of the way works best. There's no need to drag in a grand piano, marble columns, or the wall from a Tibetan temple. A small wooden box, a flat stone, or a simple shelf on the wall will be quite adequate. On this, you can arrange photographs or whatever else you would like to receive your special attention, such as a leaf or a letter from a friend. These items can be changed however it suits you. If you are particularly interested in setting up a Buddhist altar, remember to keep it simple and out of the way. You might put it in the area in which you meditate or in any place special to you, where you place things in order to see them more clearly.

Traditionally, a home Buddhist altar might have a statue of the Buddha or of Kannon (the figure representing compassion, who hears the sounds of the world's suffering). Or it might simply hold a special stone, a pine-cone, or a card on which someone's name is written. Directly in front of this central figure or object, Buddhists usually place a dish or bowl to hold offered incense. At the figure's left hand they place a candle; at its right hand, flowers, nuts, or other food offerings. But at home it is certainly OK to be less formal. Your arrangement can be as simple or as complex as you want it to be, but it will be far less distracting and much more meaningful if you keep it simple. This will be a place for you to have some time alone, where you can collect your thoughts and find a bit of peace. It's not necessary for you to dazzle yourself with your display skills or to use this as an excuse to buy that wildly overpriced antique buddha. There is a story, which many present-day Buddhist teachers love to tell, about a Zen monk who, when shivering in the freezing temperatures of his small cottage, removed the carved figure of the Buddha from the altar and used it for firewood.

When you set a place aside as being special, in most respects it's really no different from anywhere else. It is what *you* bring to this place that distinguishes it and sets it apart. If you can bring a real awareness to wherever it is you are, then the cathedral, the fancy restaurant, the storage shed, and the space under your bathroom sink will all reveal themselves to you as being equally important.

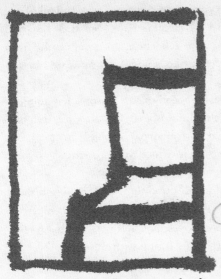

Sitting Down in the Middle of Things

To sit quietly for some period of time, in the midst of all comings and goings, has become a habit for many people. This might take the form of Zen meditation or might just be a few minutes' "time out" from the regular flow of daily activities. To stop *doing* everything and sit quietly is more difficult than it seems. There is always something calling to you that begs for your attention, some problem that needs remedying, or some pursuit that sounds a lot more interesting than just your sitting there quietly. When you try to sit still, the countless attractions of squirming and fidgeting become apparent. Your mind and body seem not to know each other and to be out of sorts. It takes practice and a certain amount of gentle self-discipline, but before long you'll find yourself looking forward to these quiet periods, when you can really be yourself. When you quiet yourself and allow other things to continue around you, the big picture slowly begins to change. Your way of looking at things becomes modified. This can be likened to the way a television picture is fragmented during transmission and then reassembled after reaching its destination.

There is a wisdom in this stopping and sitting which goes back for thousands of years. Other species have always paused this way in the midst of food gathering, nest building, or exploring new territory. And all of the world's great religious and spiritual movements have seen the value and necessity of this simple act, this pause for reflection, this brief respite from whatever agony may be confronting us, this simple and measured breath of fresh air.

Whether you sit in the formal style of Zen or just sit for a few minutes at your kitchen table, the important thing is that you sit with purpose. This does not mean that you should have any goal or object in mind, but just that you give attention to the way in which you are sitting: to your posture and to what is going on around you.

If you wish to sit formally, within the tradition of Zen Buddhism, I would certainly recommend that you find a teacher or a local sitting group in your area where beginners are always welcome and personal instruction is available. There is tremendous value in sitting with others in this way; you have an experience that no video or book can provide. Still, many people have done it on their own, at least for periods when it was the only way available. And you can learn the basic attitudes and postures from a good introductory Zen book such as Suzuki Roshi's *Zen Mind, Beginner's Mind* or the chapter titled "The Art of Zazen" in Katagiri Roshi's book *You Have to Say Something.*

There's no need for formal Zen training if all you want to do is sit quietly for a few moments, to gather your wits together, or to rest briefly behind a load of laundry or the steering wheel of the parked car. No time or place is inappropriate. Simply take a few moments, straighten your spine, relax your shoulders, and breathe normally. Nothing else matters. When you have more time, this kind of sitting can become more structured. A certain time each day can be set aside for sitting. (Mornings and evenings are both excellent for this.) If you like, you can light a candle or burn some incense. You can use a clock or kitchen timer to determine the

Sitting Down in the Middle of Things

length of your sitting, or you can just sit for as long as you're comfortable. In time, you will grow into your own particular way of sitting, just as you grow from being younger to being older. Initially, you will probably find it quite impossible to stop your mind from rambling, from running out on little collecting expeditions, sampling this daydream and that one. But just keep sitting anyway, even if it's only for a minute each morning. When thoughts rise up, just notice them and let them go. Don't make any effort to control or otherwise inhibit your thinking. Just let things calm down on their own. You'll be surprised to find things eventually falling into place. And as naturally as rain or snow, your confusing thoughts will begin to ebb, to drop off and then drift away . . . temporarily.

There really is no end to this kind of sitting. Don't expect miracles— even tiny ones—to occur. It might be better to look at this type of endeavor as a new form of exercise, a workout combining the physical and mental, a way to introduce your mind and body to each other in a different way. For many people, this practice has had great benefit, but it will be most helpful when you entertain no preconceptions regarding its results. Don't expect to suddenly become serene and carefree, or to gain the wisdom of the ages. Allow yourself to be surprised and to enjoy the changing vistas as they pass by. Try to be a good audience for whatever kind of experience reveals itself to you. But stay alert. Be ready for change. Be ready for everything. And try to let these experiences guide you as you continue on your way.

PART TWO

The Kitchen: The Raw and the Cooked

Without any goal,
the aroma of lemon peels
permeates the air.

The Art and Artlessness of Cooking

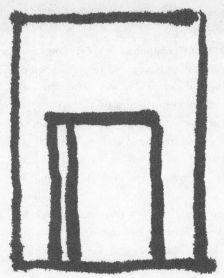

It seems that, for our entire lives, we are constantly both cooking things and being cooked, doing things and being transformed. The ingredients of our lives come to us each day, and through our actions, deeds, and thoughts, we determine how they will be best served. Each day has the potential for becoming either a rich banquet or a quick snack, depending on what we bring to the table.

Zen priest and cookbook author Edward Espe Brown says that there are essentially two styles of cooking (and of living your life). You can select a recipe or plan and then search out all the ingredients you'll need in order to produce the desired results, or you can gather what you have on hand and creatively construct something wonderful by using sincerity, spontaneity, surprise, and invention. You can, in other words, proceed with your own activity by "listening" to the ingredients and following accordingly.

There is an artistic and inventive quality inherent in the process of changing groceries into ingredients and then into food. But sometimes, something interferes with this process. Many types of cooking try to mask the natural qualities of the ingredients, and their true flavors become lost.

Each thing has its own original taste, yet it can be overwhelmed by the other things around it. The same is true of us.

Arguably, the most important student position in any Zen community is that of *tenzo,* or senior cook. This position is one that requires responsibility and dedication. And the caring and sincerity of this individual have a wide effect on the well-being of all other members of the community. Dogen was careful to articulate special instructions about this office, and his *Instructions to the Tenzo* has been widely translated and made available to students. Dogen's statements on cooking can extend into every single activity of daily life. Through his eyes, we discover the intimacy of cooking, and of being cooked.

Cooking for yourself or for others is nothing less than sharing your life. It gives you the opportunity to offer something of yourself to the world. Whether you are preparing a simple sandwich or salad, or spending hour after hour in more complex food preparation, you can enjoy the experience of giving. Even when you're alone, the aroma of a good soup steaming in the kettle adds nourishment and well-being to the entire household. As the poet Santoka (1882–1940) said, "The warmth of the food passes along from one hand to another." Each crumb of bread, each peppercorn, each bean, offers itself and is passed along to all living beings. These are the things that keep us all alive.

It is surprising how distanced many of us have become from our food. We seem to have a need for distraction even while we eat. We lose ourselves in music or conversation. When we sit in a restaurant alone, we prefer to have a newspaper or book to keep us company. We avoid looking at others. We feel an awkwardness in relating to the things we consume. We prefer that they be anonymous, coming to us fully prepared, without any hint of origin, and that they look delightful. Beyond that, we have no relationship with them. We are barely involved in what is certainly one of life's most intimate acts.

Cooking gives you the opportunity to meet the things you eat. You can touch each carrot or olive and get to know its smell and texture. You can feel its weight and notice its color and form. If it is going to become part of you, it seems worthy, at least, of acknowledgment, respect, and thanks. It takes much time and care in order for things to grow, and many labors are needed to bring these ingredients to the kitchen. There is a lot to be grateful for that takes place between the wheat field and the dumpling.

The Zen poet Ryokan (1758–1831) spent much of his life performing the ritual begging-practice known as *takuhatsu*. He would present himself at the gates and doorways of his neighbors with his rice bowl in hand. In this way, he received nourishment from the community while offering himself in return. One day after returning to his hut, he wrote, "In this one bowl, there is rice from a thousand households." When you prepare a bowl of vegetable soup, you are preparing the soup "of a thousand households." You are united with the farmers who grew the vegetables and the workers who built the roads to deliver them. You are assisted by those who manufactured the utensils and those who constructed the stove. The list is endless. And the soup, itself, will nourish not only you and your friends but all those you are yet to meet. As Suzuki Roshi said, "Preparing food is not just about yourself and others. It is about everything!"

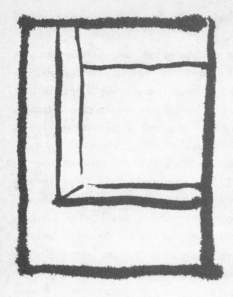

On Serving food and Eating

A recent research study found that many people exhibit the same levels of stress when hosting a dinner party as they do when preparing their income tax returns. According to the study, this stress has to do with people's fear of how they will be perceived by others. This fear of being judged is not a primary concern of most other living beings. As humans, we often seem to be bombarded by threats to our ego, and these skirmishes take up a great deal of time and often cause us to spend a great deal of money trying to defend ourselves from our own imaginations. People try to change themselves, their appearance, presentation, and setting, in order to impress others. And, apparently, more than a few people are even afraid of having others visit their home because of what might be revealed.

The Zen master Joshu was asked by a student, "What deeds should a monk properly perform?" Joshu said, "Be detached from deeds." By saying this, Joshu was not telling his student to stop doing anything. Nor was he giving an instruction to stop caring about how things were done. He was advising the student to just go forward, not trying to compile great merit, not distinguishing between good deeds and bad, in fact, not worrying about the outcome. When we do our best always, that's all we can do.

The act of serving food to others is one of utmost giving and intimacy. You share your food, your life, your time, and your experience with someone else. This kind of giving is well beyond the bounds of any kind of merit or approval one could hope for. It is complete in itself. It is its own reward.

At many temples and Zen centers, before meals, food is offered to all buddhas, hungry ghosts, animals, and beings of other realms. These small offerings are known as *saba,* or spirit offerings, and are given with great sincerity, with no expectation of recognition. They are placed carefully aside, as they would be when put before visiting guests. (There is even an old senryu [a form of poetry related to haiku] that says, "The new priest, in charge of money, is extra careful about the food offered to buddhas.")

Outside the temple walls, we find ourselves living in the land of the one-minute meal. The advertisements brag about the speed in which a "hearty meal" can be prepared. In the fast-food restaurants, we wolf down our food and ogle color photographs of an even wider array of items, eating one thing while wishing for another. It's an amazing job of salesmanship and conditioning. It's also a wonderful example of something needing to be corrected. As we know quite well, when we have one thing while wishing for another, we lose both. Again, somehow, we have lost contact with our own act of eating. At home, we eat while watching television. We seek diversion. We need to be entertained or to be distracted from this immediate and life-preserving act.

In Zen practice, there is a formal style of taking meals known as *oryoki.* This is eating reduced to its most fundamental. Everything needed is held in a small, self-contained package; small bowls that fit inside one another, a few simple utensils for eating and bowl cleaning, and a couple of pieces of cloth are all that's needed. The ritualized forms for receiving the food, for eating, and for cleanup have all been handed down from teachers to their students for centuries. The simplicity of movement allows students to give their entire attention to the act of sharing in the meal. Eating this way demands a certain concentration. There is nothing to come between the food and the act of eating. Students express gratitude to all those who grew and gathered this food and prepared it for their benefit, and to those who serve it as well. The vast majority of these providers are people who will never be known to them: the ones who planted the seeds, made the water pipes, and so on. The foods themselves have grown and prospered from generation to generation. There is a Buddhist dining hall verse for such an occasion:

> Innumerable labors brought us this food.
> We should know how it comes to us.
> Receiving this offering, we should consider.
> Whether our virtue and practice deserve it.
> Desiring the natural order of mind, we should
> Be free from greed, hate, and delusion.
> We eat to support life and to practice
> The way of the Buddha.

You might try to extend this kind of focus, this type of practice, into your own daily life. See if you can make the seat in the restaurant your own place. Consider the effort that went into your meal and think of all those who made it possible. You can even set aside a small slice of tomato or a bit of dinner roll as an offering to buddhas or to your parents or to all beings who lack the nourishment and sustenance they need. In this way, you can begin to share your meal and your compassion with others.

To sincerely serve food to guests or to yourself is, in itself, a complete and generous act. Try not to worry about how this will be perceived by others. Unless you're working as a professional chef, you'll be serving food to guests who are friends and not a panel of critics. As Dogen said, "To give something of yourself to others is a gift of priceless value, and you should do this even when no one else is watching."

The Ins and Outs of Pots and Pans

As a young child, I already knew exactly what dish washing was all about. It was about punishment—evil, torturous, and extremely unfair. I never knew why I had been singled out to suffer this excruciating, humiliating duty. I only knew that the real heroes of the world would never be caught dead having to deal with such things. With my hands in sudsy water, I envied the wealthy children of the privileged classes who, I imagined, threw away all their used dishes in the evening and bought new ones in the morning. I spent hours trying to convince my mother that our family could live a healthy life by eating only sandwiches. There was no need for us to ever dirty another dish.

Gradually, though, I changed my view. While still not enthusiastic, I began to accept the fact that doing the dishes was necessary. And in recent years I have even come to enjoy this soothing and beneficial activity. There is nothing simpler, more straightforward, or more satisfying than to be totally involved in the act of taking care of something else. Whether you are caring for another person, a coffeepot, or the manuscript of a piano sonata, you can learn how to use your whole heart. When you hold something back, when you harbor some small shade of resentment, your attitude will betray you. You will catch yourself on your own hooks. Any effort you make will feel as though it has only been half-done, and there will be no joy in it. And, in this way, your energy and spirit will both suffer.

There are not many things in the world that are less mysterious than Zen practice. When you're washing the breakfast dishes, there is no need for you to think of Zen at all. Just stick your hands in the water. You don't have to study the mysterious intermingling of air and water or the relative value of energy transformation or the emptiness of the cups and saucers or the miraculously surprising adhesive qualities of marmalade. The simplicity of the situation is captured in the following saying: The Zen master asked his student, "Have you had your rice?"

"Yes."

"Then wash your bowl."

As with most things, it helps tremendously if you can stay attuned to what you are doing. It's so easy to let your mind drift away, thinking about the great food you've just had or fast-forwarding into upcoming events in your life. But all you have to do to make your life complete and to get to the very bottom of the mystery of Zen practice is, just at this moment, to wash the dish. That's it. Wash the dish. Totally. Hold nothing back. Feel the warmth of the water. Look at the reflection of the light on the surfaces of things. Let your fingers touch the sides of the knife blade, the flat of the spatula, the rim of the dishpan. Don't think about things. These thoughts are merely distractions and diversions from what it is you're really doing. Wash the dishes. Feel what you are actually holding in your hands. Feel the genuine energy of your body as it engages in this activity.

This is not Rinzai Zen or Soto Zen. This is "Pans and Saucers Zen." There is nothing that could be more natural. As the poet Ryokan put it, "The sound of the woman scouring the cook pot blends with the sound of the frog." You are part of a larger universal activity. Whether you're rinsing out a single cup or working your way through a towering network of kettles, lids, and dishware, you can make this time enjoyable.

Notice the different materials that your dishes and utensils are made from: the iron skillets, the wooden salad bowls, plastic handles, rubber spatulas, glassware, silverware, stainless steel. Concentrate on simply washing, rinsing, and drying each spoon and plate, and you will begin to develop your own individual style of handling things. You will find your true nature beginning to emerge. You will have your own unique way of holding things, handling them, and placing them together.

For those of you who own an automatic dishwasher, you could give it a "vacation" for a while so you will really get to know your dishes by washing them by hand. Washing dishes is quite a marvelous opportunity to learn something. You have a chance to care for all these things in your life and to deliver, safely, the newly washed spoons and plates back to their drawers and cupboards. You can also care for the sink and countertops, running hot water to clear the drain, allowing the sponges and dish towels to dry in the open air. When you wash and dry a single spoon and give it your full attention, you are expressing care for the entire universe.

There is nothing more important than this kind of caring. In this way, you nurture a respect for your own life and a reverence for all the little things that keep it going. When you wash your bowl, you wash everything.

When you enter fully into this single activity, there is nothing anywhere that is not being washed. Now you can begin to experience the true joy of dish washing, which has been eluding you for so long. You may even catch a glimpse of yourself smiling, just occasionally, in the reflection of a shining plate.

Addressing the Uninvited and the Unwanted

One morning, after getting the coffee under way, I reached out toward the kitchen radio in search of the day's weather report. The clock read five-thirty, and my eyes still felt as though they were glued half-shut. Even so, I could see the line of tiny ants coming from a shiny base plate in the wall, journeying along the electrical power cord, and entering the radio through a minuscule but convenient decorative opening in its face. The ants were some of the smallest I had ever seen. And they were carrying eggs and particles of soil that were even tinier.

I remembered clearly that as a boy I had twice tried to rear ant colonies bought at the toy store, the much-advertised, "fun and educational" Ant Farms. Both times, my little farming adventures had been beset by turf warfare, hunger strikes, and devastating structural collapse. Things had not gone well. And here I was, decades later, an adult with a horde of ants setting up shop *voluntarily* inside an appliance filled with rattling news reports, car commercials, and the unrelenting variations of one of the Brandenburg Concertos.

Sometimes things have a way of moving in on us. They appear in various ways, and it's not always clear to us what their motivations or goals might be. Whether it's a mouse, a string of insects, or a visit from the building inspector, we will always find times in our lives when we are face-to-face with the unannounced and unexpected visitor. How we deal with these surprises can show us a new side of ourselves and can also be a factor in determining how we evolve into the people we become.

Having just discovered that a fair-sized community of ants was living in my radio, I tried calmly to weigh my options. My choices were as follows: (1) banish the radio (ant farm) to the outside porch, (2) aggressively attack the little community with insect spray, (3) turn the whole thing into a science project, or (4) ignore the situation and hope it would go away. The fact is, my decision was not all that well thought out. My sense of curiosity quickly overcame the initial spark of early-morning outrage that I felt at such an invasion. I knew that, without much effort, I could kill the ants and end the problem. Controlling their behavior was out of the question, but as they posed no real health concerns, being confined to the radio, I decided to go with option three; I was determined to keep an eye on them, learn why they had come to my kitchen, maybe even find out what kind of music they liked. After all, this was an opportunity I had fervently wished for when I was a nine-year-old.

And so, for a couple of months, I made a rather desultory study of their comings and goings. I made certain that there were no further incursions into other areas of the kitchen, and when I had a few extra minutes on my hands, I experimented with different radio stations and tinkered with the volume control. Nothing much seemed to change the behavior of the little denizens within. They exhibited no complaint nor showed any change in enterprise. In time, they became a little less frenetic, and I began to pay them less and less attention until, in another few weeks, I noticed suddenly that they had gone.

Whether the queen had died or they had simply become weary of their surroundings, I never learned. But I did actually feel something that I never expected under these circumstances—a sense of loss. I missed their companionship, their industry, their purpose, and their independence. Whatever else was taking place in the kitchen seemed to have no effect on the concentrated activity of their singular world. They always worked hard and did their best.

I'm certain that these ants had no intention of moving into my radio for so silly a reason as to teach me a lesson on the transitory nature of existence. But, inadvertently, that's what happened. The radio never seemed the same afterward, though it operated perfectly and without any ill effects from having been occupied. But it reminded me of some sand-worn, deserted appliance found cast up on the beach, an abandoned relic which had once contained life but was now just a hollow shell.

In telling this story, I'm not suggesting that we should welcome all manner of insects and vermin into our homes. We must do what we can to protect our own health and the health of our families. The Zen teacher Robert Aitken, who lives on the "big island" of Hawaii, has often commented on the ordeal of sharing his living quarters with cockroaches. After decades of coping with this problem, he now kills them as he encounters them—with Buddhist compassion—wishing them "better luck next time."

Addressing the Uninvited and the Unwanted

It's easy for most of us to react quickly to something unpleasant. Not only do we kill all household pests, but we toss our garbage to the winds without thinking. However, our first instinct is not always our only choice. Zen tells us that there is nothing in our life that can be hurled away. There is no vile corner to which we can consign pests, garbage, or unwanted experiences. We can attempt to deal with these problems, but we cannot pretend that they don't exist.

On the western shore of New York's Staten Island, there is a monument memorializing people's desire to hurl things away. It is a mountain known as "Fresh Kills"—nearly six hundred feet high and covering over two thousand acres. It is the largest landfill in the world and can be seen from space with the naked eye. There are other, smaller, mountains similar to this one growing all over the world. Although all phenomena are endlessly arising and disappearing, it will take a long time to erase mountains such as these.

In the past, most people had fewer possessions than now, and what they owned was cared for in a different way. The idea of possessions being disposable was not ingrained in us until the early twentieth century. The cause for this change was largely a matter of business tactics. Men such as K. C. Gillette discovered that it was more profitable to sell their customers a continuous supply of "disposable" items—like razors—than it was to sell them one that was long-lasting. Today, there are disposable eating utensils, diapers, cameras, paintbrushes, and many other items not considered valuable enough to keep. We use them once and then forget them. We don't know where they come from, and we don't care where they go. They all end up on the mountain.

We often seem immune to the gross indignity of waste in our lives. We've been trained to consume and discard, rather than to take care of what we already have. And this can extend to our relationships with other people, our view of our environment, and our image of ourselves. If something becomes boring or too difficult, we attempt to toss it away, to pretend it never existed, to find something better or more exciting. It becomes easier for us to try to rid ourselves of difficulties than to learn from them. We keep adding more to the mountain.

As I look back to that early morning, when I first discovered the ants in my house, I can recall thinking briefly of killing them; if there had been more of them or they had been near our food, I would have. But I'm glad I didn't follow my first impulse. I'm glad I didn't throw away the opportunity of watching them awhile. In some small measure, giving my initial reaction another consideration afforded me an opportunity I wouldn't have otherwise had. (It is wise sometimes to let things happen by themselves. When you do plan to intervene there is wisdom in considering the effects your actions will have on yourself and others.)

An ant is an awfully small item when compared to something that can be seen from space with the naked eye; but when we kill one without full consideration, we are jettisoning some small part of ourselves. We are throwing one more thing onto the already existing mountain.

Infinite Winter, Timeless Summer

When things are running smoothly, the refrigerator is very much like some people's idea of the perfect Zen student. It is calm, cool, and quiet, and it possesses its own inner light.

Actually, the refrigerator is quite a noble thing on its own merit. For many of us, it has a formidable presence. It offers consistency, dependability, and long-lasting service. Even when we cover it with magnets and memos, and kick and slam its doors, it allows us to enjoy many good foods that might otherwise become spoiled. When we are hungry, we go to the refrigerator. That much, we know. But do we ever give this appliance one moment's thought during any other time of the day or night? Like many things, we take the hardworking refrigerator for granted.

Dogen once stated, "The activities within the house just move along their way, with only the furnishings of spring, autumn, winter, and summer." The seasons of the year enhance and invigorate the places where we live. And there is one place in our home where it is eternally winter. The refrigerator has another fascinating quality: It uses heat and energy to produce coolness. The Buddhist texts on nonduality address this seeming contradiction; there is no light without darkness, no cold without heat. Just as things in the home sometimes need to be heated, they also need to be cooled, and cool temperatures are one of the mildest and most basic forms of food preservation.

For all its value, your refrigerator doesn't need much when it comes to maintenance. You clean its handles and wipe off the outside surfaces with a damp cloth. Periodically, you clean off the coils, wipe up the interior spills, and remove any contents that have become undesirable. Not much more is needed. As you do this minimal cleaning, you might think for a moment about the poet Shinkei (1406–75), who thought that nowhere in the world was there anything more beautiful than or as exquisite as ice.

Throughout Zen's history, many writings have investigated the differences between ice and water (different forms of the same thing) or have attempted to find the place in one's life where there is neither heat nor cold. There are many stories, also, of monks sitting *zazen* in the wild rain and snow outside their huts and temples. And the feeling of becoming settled, which one sometimes experiences during meditation, has itself been compared to falling snow. Another poet, Socho (fifteenth–sixteenth centuries) once likened the illuminating qualities of this type of snow to those of frozen moonlight.

If the refrigerator is the place in the home that houses an eternal winter, the stove is surely the source of everlasting summer. It offers warmth and well-being. It is a place of transformation, changing the raw materials of yeast and flour, harvested fruits and honey, into something entirely different. We always look forward to seeing what will come out of the oven. And we are always a little amazed when everything works the way we expected. There is often a certain edge of mystery to baking and cooking. We are not completely comfortable trusting our appliances this way. Still, we do it. And most of the time, the results please us. The oven is a wonderful example of controlled energy, and it allows us to produce pleasing and well-prepared food. Suzuki Roshi said that in order to bake good bread, we must do it over and over, until we *become* bread. We must put ourselves into the oven, just as we put ourselves into everything else that we do. It is only then that we know what bread is and what we are.

Recently, I literally put myself into the oven when I tackled the formidable task of cleaning this appliance. It struck me that cleaning the oven may be the closest we can come, at least at home, to laboring in hell. The only difference, it seemed to me, was that the heat was turned off. Before me was an evil, blackened crust—all that remained of countless breads, casseroles, fruit pies, melted cheeses, bubbling juices, happily spattering olive oil, and innumerable meals that had been heated and reheated a thousand times. This residue was lifeless, cold, charred, and foreboding. It seemed to challenge me directly. It dared me to clean it. It did everything but smirk.

So I dragged out newspapers, gloves, putty knives and chisels, steel wool and rags, and arranged them neatly on the floor. Then I remembered Soko, one of many Japanese temple gods, who is in fact the kitchen god in charge of the oven. His job is to protect goodness and to avert catastrophes caused by those who innocently chip and scrape in his realm.

Feeling somewhat protected from raging, supernatural forces, I began cleaning the racks and sidewalls, and then got down close and confronted the dark corners. As I scraped away the many layers of grit and carbon, I tried to imagine how life would be without this oven. In the days before people built houses, they had already become intimate with fire. The campfire became their portable home. People depended upon fire for cooking, as well as to protect and warm themselves. And fire also served an important role as friend and companion to these people. As new materials and new technologies were discovered, and later refined, people no longer had to chase around after firewood in order to bake their bread.

You may be a person who jumps right up and cleans your oven immediately after using it. Not me. I reserve oven cleaning for very special occasions, such as leap year and the like. But when I do it, I try to do it well.

When you clean your oven, it is best to allow yourself plenty of time, and to get to know all its surfaces and inner workings. When you clean the top of your stove, you can consider the perfect circles of the burners, the transience of the flame, the removal of smoke into the atmosphere by the fan, and the way time changes the warm into the cold. You can ask yourself what an oven really is and how it got here; you can reflect on the ways your life is partnered with nature, the immeasurable number of living things around you, the ores from deep in the earth from which the oven is made, and the electricity or gas that serves as fuel.

When you're down on the floor, surrounded by newspapers and covered in soot, you have the perfect opportunity to directly encounter something that has passed through countless burnings, seasoned by a thousand steaming meals, and tested by your home's most extreme conditions. You can wipe the ashes from your brow, kiss your bloodied knuckles, and continue cutting through the darkness. You can consider the real meaning of the word *self-cleaning*.

While you may be a novice at pondering the mysteries of heat and fire, this topic runs throughout the history of Zen. Some Zen teachers describe the past as ash, the future as fuel, and the present moment as fire. But the great masters such as Dogen Zenji were quick to point out that there is no separation among the three. There is no separation between past, present, and future. And firewood and ash are, themselves, not separate. Each thing is complete this very moment. Takeda Shingen, who practiced Zen in the sixteenth century, compared human life to "a snowflake on a blazing stove." And his teacher, Kwaisen, said, "If you wish to meditate peacefully, there is no need for you to go where there are mountains and streams; When your thoughts are quiet, fire itself is quite cool and refreshing." Today's Zen teachers like to compare students to firewood, explaining that the dry, seasoned students help those who are newer and greener to warm to their practice. (Of course, it's also true that those who are new help the older ones as well. They bring their enthusiastic questions and energy to this practice, and keep it vibrant and alive.)

There are many kinds of heat in our lives, and many forms of burning. Wood burns; propane burns; coal burns. The star at the center of our solar system burns, as does the core of the earth we live on. Our own bodies burn calories of energy in order to maintain their healthy existence. Sometimes we burn with fever or anger. When we consider it appropriate, we burn incense as an offering of purification. And after we die, in many cases our bodies are cremated.

Yet despite the multitude of ways that we and the world around us burn, we can seek—and find—an underlying unity. The centuries-old collection of writing known as the *Zenrin Segoshu* informs its readers that individual pieces of broken and burning wood exhibit an unlimited variety of forms, yet the smoke emitted is all of one form. To understand this "one form," to experience "fire itself as quite cool and refreshing," it's sometimes helpful to reflect quietly on the calmness centered within your own activity. You can experience cool resolve in just keeping your chimney clean, caring for ashes, clearing vents and furnace filters, and in conserving energy.

It's never too late to begin this type of practice. Sometimes firewood itself comes into bloom and branches out, even though it has already been cut and stacked for burning.

PART THREE

The Bedroom, Bath, and Washroom

This April morning,

the shadow of a faucet

seems to be blooming.

On the Many Intricacies of Water

All life is intimately connected to water. The major component of the human body and of the surface of the planet Earth is water. Without water, all life would cease. Yet many people take this wondrous resource for granted, knowing only that "this one's hot, that one's cold." Most of us don't get personally involved with installing or maintaining our own home plumbing systems. Once in a while we might have to change a washer or tighten a fitting or free a clogged drain. But mostly, we don't need to overly concern ourselves with the mysterious interconnectedness of flow systems, pipes, elbows, traps, drains, water heaters, showerheads, overflows, downspouts, male and female couplings, plugs, holding tanks, septic systems, pumps, sumps, and sinks. But it might be beneficial for us to take a look at *some* of this complexity and to examine our relationship to, and reliance on, water.

Dogen tells us, "All streams come from a single source." And science has shown that the amount of water in the world has always remained constant. (The volume of the earth's waters is around 1.5 billion cubic kilometers.) The water that we use today has been recycled on a regular basis since the origin of the planet, following the natural laws of evaporation, filtration, condensation, precipitation, and so forth. Air and water are the two most indispensable factors in our lives, and yet we take them for granted. Luckily for us, there are others who constantly monitor their quality and availability.

When D. H. Lawrence moved to the southwestern United States, he became more interested in water than he had been during earlier periods of his life. He spent quite a bit of time thinking about it, and once wrote, "Water is H_2O, hydrogen two parts, oxygen one. But there is also a third thing that makes it water and nobody knows what that is."

The qualities of water have been remarked upon for centuries by Zen teachers everywhere. The larger Japanese temples all had a person in residence who was known as the *suiju*, or manager of the water. Good water, like food, was a crucial component in the health and well-being of all temple residents. *Seikasui* was the name given to water taken from the well between the hours of two and four in the morning. This water was considered especially pure and was handled in a different manner. Its character was studied thoroughly.

The study of water is one of eternal interest, yet it seems, still, to be almost indefinable.

We envy water's flexibility and freedom, and the way it flows around its obstacles and follows its own natural path. In its pure state, water has no color of its own. Having no innate shape, it borrows the form of whatever is around it; in a square container, it is square, and in a round one, round. It adheres to itself, and when turned to steam, can rise above itself. It is vastly adaptable, and when frozen into ice, it can even float upon itself. It's compact, virtually as compressed as things can get. It manifests itself in a myriad of ways. Dogen tells us that it is the home of both fish and dragons, and that its freedom depends on nothing but itself. He urges us to pay particular attention to the ways in which it is conveyed and how it behaves under different conditions. At the San Francisco Zen Center, Shunryu

Suzuki Roshi stressed to his students that water be treated as a living thing, and that "true nature is watching water." By watching water, you really begin to understand the distinctions between stillness and motion, between something and nothing, the inside and outside, the obvious and the subtle. You learn about stream diverting, going with the flow, and the uses and effects of pressure.

Try to appreciate the vast system of lines and connections that brings your life flowing to you from the lakes and reservoirs, ponds and potholes of your own experience. Allow your life to take on its own natural shape and color. Try to see yourself as flowing. Sense the subtle ways in which you turn off and then release the taps of energy and emotion residing inside you, the ways in which you direct and control your movements, the tidelike rise and fall of your limits and capacities, and the periodic comfort of settling into your own stillness.

Those who have witnessed a flood or a crashing coastal storm are quite familiar with the immensity and overwhelming capabilities of water's power. Yet all of us have also seen its refreshing mists and gentle vapors, its morning dewdrops and multicolored arches. There is a wisdom to be found in water, whether we see it revealed in a partial rainbow or in a clotted, oil-spotted, roadside culvert. Water seems always to know what it is and where it is. It is unmoving, yet it travels everywhere. It is clear, yet it reflects all things. Just one small drop of it is sufficient to contain the reflection of the entire moon. Perhaps, if we look closely, we can see this moon, and many other things as well.

The Smallest Rooms in Your House

Bathrooms and washrooms are sometimes separate and sometimes the same place. If that doesn't sound like a Zen saying, I don't know what does. But let's take things one step at a time. Let's consider, first, the shower and bath. Is there anyone who doesn't feel better after taking a shower or bath? It helps us feel refreshed and invigorated.

The communal life of the early Zen monasteries necessitated a practical and expeditious kind of bathing, which is still found today in modern Zen communities where students live together. Bathing was always considered a necessity, not a retreat or minivacation, and there were strict rules governing the use of the bath.

These were the days before hand soap, and cleanliness was achieved only through rigorous scrubbing, using limited amounts of hot water, old rags, and pumice. Not until Japan's government realized how isolated the nation had become, and opened trade with the Western world, during the Meiji Restoration of 1868, did hand soap start to be used on a regular basis. Zen teachers found this new soap to be a good teaching tool. "Zen is like soap," they said, "first you use it to clean yourself, then you must wash it away." And it was pointed out that soap is capable of cleaning itself, and that it is the nature of soap to disappear in the process.

Today, many of us have access to both modern showers and bathtubs. (A friend of mine once derogatorily referred to this as the option between "resting beneath falling water or stewing in your own juice.") Whichever you choose, there comes a time for washing off the dust of the world, for revealing yourself to yourself. And you might consider the way others relate to water and bathing: The homeless search for water constantly; healthy animals and children frolic in the water; caretakers of the incapacitated and infirm bathe their charges gently. You can treat the tubs and sinks and surrounding walls and floors kindly. When you're finished, you can wipe the fixtures dry, hang the towels carefully, and make certain that no water is left running. In these ways, you are planting seeds of appreciation, even in the tile and porcelain. These little details can be of monumental significance. They are the moments that are your life. They are time. There is no need for any added glamour. (The origin of the word *glamour* is found in ancient Scotland, where it meant "having the illusion of beauty where there is none.") Thanks to soap and water, we can all now be beautiful. Suzuki Roshi always taught his students to be thankful for water. "After we wash," he said, "we always empty the water towards, rather than away from, our body. This shows our respect for the water."

In the year 1239, Dogen wrote explicit instructions to his students on how they were to bathe, groom themselves, and care for the washrooms and toilets of the monastery. The temple toilet was called the *Tosu,* and the instructive essay on its care was entitled *"Senjo."* In the course of these instructions, Dogen reminded his followers that "even the Buddha had a toilet." This is a fact that many people choose to ignore.

Westerners, especially, have always seemed to consider the toilet as some secret, inner sanctum—the less said about it, the better. When they *do* speak about it, they often use euphemistic terms such as those employed when speaking of sexual perversion or death. If speaking about the toilet is so difficult, what about actually *cleaning* it? Throughout the history of Zen, cleaning the toilet has been considered a time-honored chore, and the task was often assigned to senior students. It helped reinforce the idea that there are no impure places, and that, as Bodhidharma, the first patriarch of Zen in China, put it, "the universe is a vast emptiness and there is nothing holy about it." One place is really no different, no better or worse, than any other.

The fact is, the toilet is an excellent symbol of our humanity. Moreover, the elimination of waste products is a feature common to all living beings. What we take in, we must burn or expel. All we have to do is keep our mind clear and stay out of our own way. It's as simple as that.

Many people have an aversion to cleaning the toilet. If you're one of them, you might consider asking yourself the following questions: How did I get this aversion? Are there valid reasons behind it? Research has shown that the area surrounding the kitchen sink has much more harmful bacteria than does the average toilet rim. Still, you may have qualms about cleaning it. Try approaching this work with a different spirit. After all, a toilet is a wonderful thing to have when you need it. Just try imagining your life without it. And the next time you begin to clean it, try approaching it in a more grateful way, taking it less for granted. As you scrub away, you can wish for all beings to be cleansed of impurities, greed, anger, and delusion. And you can again express your gratitude for the food that keeps you alive, and for your own body's internal plumbing, which processes this food before filtering, separating, and discarding its waste.

All of this takes very little time. First check the toilet paper, soap, towel, and cleaning brush. Then scrub out the bowl and wipe the surfaces of the lid and seat. Finally, rinse and wipe off the sink. By straightening and cleaning the room, you make it pleasant for the next visitor, even when you live alone. If you feel like it, you can offer fresh flowers or burn a stick of incense.

As you do these everyday chores around the house, you have the perfect opportunity to engage in what some people refer to as integrative practice. This is just another way of saying that you try to bring the qualities of *zazen,* sitting meditation, into your everyday activities. The laundry or washroom offers another venue where you can experience this practice. It's just as natural for us to clean and care for the clothes we wear as it is for an egret to preen his feathers or for a house cat to lick her fur in the sunshine. Most people these days don't have to beat their clothing against river rocks or rinse them in their drinking pools. Doing the laundry can in fact be a very pleasant experience; it's a great chance to enjoy a feeling of renewal. Consider the warmth of the laundry that comes out of the dryer, the feel of each item as you fold it. If you use a clothesline to dry your laundry, you can also marvel at the warmth of the sun and the release of moisture into the air. Savor the aroma of freshness in the things you have washed. Consider the nature of the things before you and of those who made them available.

In formal Zen practice, there are explicit instructions on how to care for one's robes and bedding. Each item is handled in a certain way, washed in a certain way, and stored in a certain way, all handed down through the centuries from teacher to student. These small rituals have a twofold purpose: They help ensure uniformity and equality in the monastery setting, and they also help residents focus their attention on what they're doing. The point is not to do things quickly but to do them completely. X

Today, we often sacrifice many of life's experiences for the sake of speed.

We're constantly short of time, no matter how much time we have. We're continually preparing for and rushing to meet "something." What this "something" is, we often don't know. We only know that we have to be ready for it, and the sooner we escape from what it is we are doing, the better. But once we step back a bit and begin to look at things more carefully, we can begin asking the questions of ourselves that can instruct our lives.

Even when confronted with the most modern and shining coin-operated machines at the Laundromat, you can find the subtle questions and teachings of Zen. But sometimes it is best not to take these questions and symbols so seriously. After all, just how permanent is "permanent press"? And what about the machine on the wall dispensing "change"? You can view the spinning drums of the commercial dryers as prayer wheels, or wheels of Samsara. You can ask if bleach will really make white things whiter, or if the "gentle cycle" makes the machine become more compassionate. And what should you do when your entire load of washing becomes "unbalanced"?

Just do your laundry and try not to identify yourself too much with your own clothing. As Suzuki Roshi said, we sometimes talk about the clothes we wear, and we sometimes talk about our human bodies, but neither of these is really what we are. We are "the big activity." This big activity can also be the small activity. It can be the loose button bouncing against the leg of the table. It can be the mending and patching of clothing, the washing of one's work clothes, or the smell of clean socks folded in a drawer. It can often be as simple as hearing the sound of water dripping on other water.

A World of Mirrors

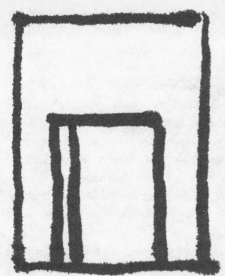

The earliest mirror was nothing more than a reflecting pool of water, and the glass mirrors of today may still occasionally be compared by poets to vertical surfaces of water. Others see mirrors as a necessity, a way of verifying one's condition or establishing one's sense of place.

Zen teachers have always used the image of a mirror to represent the enlightened mind. The polished surface of the mirror reflects outwardly, with no distortion, interference, judgment, or hesitation. It illuminates everything placed before it, but doesn't analyze, evaluate, or worry about the state of things. It simply reflects life, without trapping or holding on to it.

When you look into a mirror, you see the reflection of your own face, but you are unable to see the reflection of your thoughts. Suzuki Roshi said that our eyes can see only the things outside ourselves, the objective things, and that if we reflect too much on ourselves, that "self" ceases to be our true self. If we look with our mind and heart, and not just with our eyes, we discover the brightest kind of mirror. In it, everything is reflected.

The number of mirrors you have in your home may indicate something about your own personality. Those who are vain may have a reflecting surface on every wall, but for most of us, one mirror is plenty. We use it for grooming and for quick referral from time to time. A mirror is not really necessary to most of our lives, yet few people disdain having them altogether. We seem to be fascinated by ourselves and the way in which we might appear to others. It's no accident that the walls of many bars and restaurants are lined with mirrors.

It's good for us to keep in mind that these images are not really us. They are only the play of reflected light. They are an optical rebound, a visual echo. That's all. The poet Yoka said, "Mind is thought and objects are set against it: the two are like marks on the surface of the mirror. When dirt is removed, the light begins to shine. Both mind and objects are forgotten, and true nature is revealed." Finding this true nature is the ultimate quest of the Zen student, whether through conscious effort or fortunate occurrence. We try to wipe away the illusions that interfere with seeing our true selves.

When you practice meditation, you open yourself to the possibility of seeing what has always been there. You practice not interjecting your "self" into things, but rather identifying with them. You try to look at everything honestly and compassionately, without blinders or filters, and to wend your way through the obstacles you encounter without bumping into them or becoming stuck to them. You try to get out of your own way.

I remember once watching a Golden-crowned Sparrow fling itself repeatedly against a darkened window. It was defending its territory and was doing battle against its own reflection. Again and again, it threw its body against the glass until it was quite exhausted. It is often the same with people. Our imagined thoughts and irrational fears have us behaving in self-destructive ways. We create fantasies that would rival those of any writer of fiction. We join Alice in going through the looking glass and become all that we see reflected rather than what we really are.

The Zen priest Shotetsu (fourteenth–fifteenth century) often told students of his constant struggle to keep from writing someone else's poems.

The mirror reminds us that we too must struggle, to keep from living someone else's life.

Tending the Place Where You Sleep

We seem to have a natural curiosity about other people's sleeping arrangements. When visiting museums or historical sites, we curious trespassers spend a great deal of time congregating near the beds of the famous, entirely captivated, totally intrigued. There is actually something very moving about viewing these sleeping places, where the people were most vulnerable, most themselves. Even though the beds may not have been slept in for the past hundred years or so, there remains a sense of intimacy and immediacy about them.

We all have our place to rest, whether it is in a baroque, canopied, sequestered chamber or in a dirty sleeping bag beneath the freeway overpass. Sleeping is one of the fundamentals of any life, and the Lotus Sutra (one of the treatises based on the teachings of Buddha) refers to bedding, along with food, medicine, and clothing, as one of the Four True Offerings that can be given to others. It is one of the true gifts that can make a difference between life and death.

When you go to bed, you surrender yourself to a totally new environment, an intimate sector that contains possibilities for rest, love, birth, and death. It's the one place where you are completely vulnerable and unguarded. Even if you sleep with another, you eventually withdraw into your own private self, and the bed becomes the place where you make the transition from being conscious to unconscious and back again. The edges of the bed contain the borders of your sleep. You let go of everything you know, and trust in some greater power to keep you safe and protected until morning.

When I was a young boy, I asked my mother, "How far can we go in our dreams and still get back in time to wake up?" This was quite a joke around our house for a long time afterward, but thinking about it now, I wonder if this wasn't a telltale sign of my nascent interest in Buddhism. We Buddhists are always desperately, fervently, trying to wake ourselves up. And it is little consolation to learn that Dogen once said, "Even in sleep, we continue our practice."

The temple priests and monks were provided with a wide variety of mats and cushions—zafus, futons, zabutons, and the like—in order to practice "sitting and lying-down Zen." The traveling monks and hermits who headed out on their own considered the entire outside landscape to be their home. They spoke of using "the stone as a pillow, the sky as a blanket." Even today, we can consider the place where we sleep as a kind of landscape—the broad fields of the blankets, the hill-like pillows.

As you air out your own sheets and blankets, you can be grateful for the fresh-smelling aroma and sunshine that permeate them. As you plump the pillows, try to remember the dreams that were born upon them. And when folding quilts, you can recall the robes of the "patchwork monks" who slept enveloped in the smell of pine trees. The sewing of these robes was described by one monk as "the sewing of one cloud to another." This is the way our lives are put together, one piece, one moment at a time.

As you smooth the wrinkles from the top layer of bedding, you can consider the waking world. What does it mean to come fully alive? How do you change as you prepare to go out and encounter others? What do you leave behind? Now that you are embarked on your life again, it is the bed's opportunity to rest. Perhaps you can take some of its comfort with you. As you leave the bedroom, you might offer a slight bow, or *gassho,* hands palm to palm before your face, as a small offering of thanks. We are all most grateful for this period of rest and quiet. But as Katagiri Roshi told his students, "Now it's time to wake up! Your life must be rooted in the real earth, not in sleep."

PART FOUR

Outside Surroundings

This late August day—

    together on the same branch,

        dead leaves and live ones.

Raking Leaves, Trimming Branches, Moving Stone

In many homes, it takes just a few steps to go from the interior to the area outside. So it's only natural to continue sweeping and tidying up in the out-of-doors, tending the entryways, paths, and adjacent grounds. In some ways there is very little difference be-tween sweeping the floor and raking the yard. At many Japanese Zen temples, raking is followed by sweeping the paths and grounds with special straw brooms. Temple in-structors often tell their students that one's entire life is just "sweeping the garden."

There are ways in which sweeping and raking differ, and they range from the obvious (one is usually done indoors, the other outside) to the more subtle (one emphasizes removal, the other reunification). Both of these activities are considered essential to the everyday work-practice of Zen students. From centuries ago, the *enju,* or garden manager, was the one in charge of overseeing outdoor work. Some effort was made to give an overall impression of order and care, yet things were not to appear overly cared for or artificially arranged. The tea master Rikyu (sixteenth century) stated that whenever guests were expected, the leaves should be swept a few hours before the time of arrival. And that if fallen leaves were to collect after that, they should be left alone. Only an unaccomplished host would leave the ground bare of leaves entirely. There also were instructions on how to use the leaves, stones, and pebbles that accumulated after raking. The leaves were used as compost or as kindling to heat the bathwater. Stones and gravel were placed in depressions in the earth as leveling agents or pressed into the areas beneath rain gutters. It was mandatory that nothing go to waste, that nothing be thrown away. And students were again instructed on the differences between "letting go of things" and trying to hide or discard the unwanted elements of their lives.

There is both joy and melancholy in the raking of autumn leaves. On the one hand, you experience an exuberance at being outside in the fresh air, listening to the wind, and seeing the vivid colors of the season. On the other, you feel sad because another year is coming to an end, and because you're reminded of the transitoriness of all things in the natural world.

As you do the job of raking, you may find that the type of rake you use has an influence on your attitude and the way you work. While using the steel rake, you may have an inclination to dig in a little deeper, looking beneath the larger pebbles and tumbled stones. You may grow more light-hearted and exhibit a certain bounciness or flair while using the bamboo rake, a tool with a certain liveliness that even the broom does not possess. Eventually, you may begin to get a new sense of the space around you, becoming more aware of the rake itself and the gaps it has between its working parts. You can see that because it is designed this way, it can't achieve its finished work all at once, that some things manage to "get away."

Even when there are no leaves, the raking by the monks continues. The sand surrounding the stone gardens is raked into the shape of ocean waves. The garden plots are raked and cared for. There is always much work to do. But one can expect, also, to be interrupted, to catch a glimpse of nature's sense of play. When a sudden gust of wind scatters a pile of leaves, one's initial sense of dismay gives way to the insight that the wind is just another form of rake, another spirit busied with arranging and restoring things to its own fashion.

Whether working in the yard or just going about the daily business of life, you are continually adjusting, trimming, touching, shaping, and tinkering with the wealth of things around you. It may be difficult for you to know when to stop. We are all torn between the extremes of taking care of things and leaving them alone, and we question whether many things could ever get along without us. We find ourselves with pruning shears in hand, snipping away at this or that, telling ourselves that we're only being helpful, redefining something else's space, removing that which is unappealing to us. It's not that we really want to change the world. We just want to fix it up slightly. We'd like to lose a few pounds or rid ourselves of some small habit. Maybe we'd like to help a friend improve his situation or repair a few loose ends in the lives of our children. All of this shaping and controlling can have an adverse affect. Unlike someone skilled in the art of bonsai gardening, we may *unintentionally* stunt much natural growth before it occurs. We could be in danger of pruning many of our own good qualities away. And our meddling may not be appreciated by others. Most things will get along superbly without our editing, fussing, and intervention. We can learn to just let them be. As a poem of long ago puts it, "In the landscape of spring, the flowering branches grow naturally, some are long, some are short."

Human control of and interference with the more traditional methods of agriculture have led to the scientific development of many domestic plants and animals that can no longer reproduce without our help or exist in an unsupervised environment. This is plainly staggering to comprehend. Sometimes there is real need for us to question how much of this is improvement and how much of it is folly. How much pruning do you do before you begin to prune yourself away? How much tinkering can things stand before they are turned into other entities totally?

One of the universal symbols of Zen study is the image of the full moon. This moon symbolizes great realization or enlightenment. When rendered in paintings or other visual arts, the moon is usually accompanied by a few scattered branches of a tree or shrub. This serves two purposes: It helps to keep the moon (our clear realization) in perspective, and it also reminds us that this realization is rooted here on Earth and not isolated and banished into distant space. The moon, the branch, and ourselves have much in common. We all grow naturally and show variations: Some of us are long, some short, some bright, and some dark. We all bloom in our own good time. As the Zen teachers tell us, there is no reason to tear open the branch in search of the cherry blossoms. Each thing appears in its own time and place.

When we study the leaves and branches of Zen, we acknowledge our own judgment, our own aesthetics, and our own training. But we also learn to stop trying to manipulate everything and simply "let go" of it all. Rather than occupying ourselves with the many things in our lives over which we have no control, we can concentrate on those matters that truly demand our attention, that call to us and deserve our care. There are even a few things that need to be gently snipped, bundled up, and removed. But when our pruning is concluded, it's time to relax and enjoy the many-budded branches of our lives, the stubborn weeds and nodding flowers before us.

But what about lawns? Lawns can be a problem. Even if you do not have one, you can enter into the "koan of the lawn," which asks: "Is a lawn a 'natural' thing or an 'unnatural' one?" Actually, I have never seen the word *lawn* anywhere in the history of Zen literature. *Grass* is something else altogether. Green grass, long grass, winter grass, a blade of grass, wild grass, and the hundreds and thousands of other grasses all appear in poetry and written teachings. But nowhere is there much encouragement for those who mow lawns. The closest thing I could find was a brief poem by Konishi Raizan (1654–1716). He wrote, "I pick and gather, and then discard, the new spring grass." This sounds to me like an activity dangerously close to lawn mowing. And it raises questions: What are the reasons, guidelines, and laws that govern the mowing of lawns? Who sets the standards? Is it all about the social pressures of conforming? Is it good for the grass?

If you're about to mow your own lawn, you might consider asking for the help of Doji, the guardian of Buddhist temple grounds and buildings. Perhaps, with his help, you could better understand the reasons and techniques for grass cutting. You might ask yourself about uniformity, blending in, stewardship, and culture. You might learn about cultivating a field that produces no crop, and begin to see borders and edges and boundaries in a different light. The world is filled with standing and falling grasses, with myriad things arising and fading before our eyes. Only the grass knows how green it can ever be or how tall it can ever grow. The *Zenrin Segoshu*, a fifteenth-century collection of Zen writings, says that even in the dew on a tiny blade of nameless grass, the moon will show itself.

When you mow your lawn, mow it with every fiber of your being. Listen to the sound of the mower, smell the sweet aroma in the air, and look for the moon in the cut grass clinging to the bottoms of your shoes. There are many kinds of grasses in our lives, and the moon has many ways of revealing itself.

As we continue our outside tasks, we may find ourselves working with elements less pliant and forbearing than weeds and blades of grass.

For many years now, my wife and I have been giving periodic attention to a stone retaining wall that graces one small corner of our property. Only about three feet high, the wall was built with a great deal of care by the previous owner, probably as a long, weekend project. The stones, almost without doubt, came from the surrounding land and are of rather poor quality: graywacke, chert, shale, and other undifferentiated, sedimentary conglomerates. They were placed in position and pasted together with generous dollops of ready-mixed concrete, and for many years and through much bad weather they adequately served the purpose of holding back the hilly, clay-based yard above it, saving it from collapse.

But gradually, the wall began to lean. Ever so slowly, we started to notice that the wall seemed to be distancing itself from the ground next to it. It pulled away cautiously, as if trying to see what would happen. There was no violence, no upheaval, no jarring of the Richter scale, just a barely perceptible peeling away from things adjacent, a gentle, steady move to be alone.

And, as is the case with most things, the leaning ultimately became more pronounced. Whether due to inordinately heavy winter rains or to some hidden character flaw, the wall curled away from its neighboring soil as if repulsed. For many months we watched this strange development, hoping that it would stop of its own accord. But the wall continued to lean out over its homemade base, beyond anyone's idea of an angle of repose, until the force of gravity brought a small section of it crashing down onto our driveway.

As my wife and I began the task of dismantling and rebuilding our stone bulwark, I thought about the tiny marine worm that makes its home in the eelgrass communities of Tomales Bay, not far from where we live. By anyone's standard, this small animal, which measures not much more than two inches in length, is an exceptional creature. It is one of the most excellent practitioners of masonry to be found on Earth.

While we wrestled stones from the grip of compacted clay and tight-fisted mortar, I entertained my wife with tales of the marine worm. I told her of how it builds a tubular dwelling, with grains of sand, surrounding itself in a narrow, elongated cone, perfectly straight-sided and as smooth as glass inside, each tiny grain fitting exactly against the side of the grain next to it, and just one sand grain's thickness from beginning to end. There is often a bit of rearranging and substitution involved as the worm makes subtle changes in its selection, trying to find a perfect fit, nudging the more stubborn particles into place, choosing one bit of material over another, seeking an ideal marriage of line and facet, of hollows, hillocks, and con-cavities. And after rubbing the interior of its delicate shell several times in order to ensure a glasslike finish, the artisan settles, upside down, to live out the rest of its life in the sand.

As we worked with pry bars clanging, levering out the unwanted sec-tions of wall, and chipping old concrete blisters from the stone with sharply pointed hammers, I thought about the peaceful, protected waters where this quiet creature lives, the wind-borne ripples overhead, and the terns riding the breezes up higher still. This isolated worker, which has found design and usefulness in the things surrounding it, was a source of inspiration for me. But at the same time, it made me aware of my own human awkwardness. I envied the worm's diligence and ingenuity yet real-ized how senseless this kind of envy is.

Looking back on that day, I can see that my thoughts were interfering with the work at hand. Dogen once said that when we intellectualize too much about our actions, we are "planting our flowers on top of stones." It is enough that we tend to the walls, rake the leaves, and turn the garden soil. Working outside offers us a great opportunity for seeing a different aspect of the place we live. When we enter the landscape with directness and simplicity, both *awkwardness* and *inspiration* become useless words. And sometimes we find ourselves there—lost deep within the heart of the work.

Adventures in Light and Darkness

I remember one late-summer afternoon, sitting high up on the gently pitched front section of our roof. My wife and I had spent the greater part of the past two days removing and discarding the worn, deteriorating shingles, which no longer held off the winter rains. We had also pulled out and pried up thousands of nails and steel staples from the plywood underneath, trying to salvage what we could, and hoping that the entire roof would not need replacing. We did not know, at the time, that the work we were doing was futile, that the plywood roof, along with all the shingles, would need replacing after all. But when I think back on this particular afternoon, I can still feel the warmth of the sun and smell the sweet aroma of newly exposed wood.

The work we had done was valuable, even though it had no outward importance or bearing on the end result. It could easily have been considered a waste of time, doing something that would only have to be done over again. Yet there seemed to be a kind of joy in losing ourselves to the labor and to the summer breezes far above the ground. We were as content and purposeful on our splintered roof as we could have been anywhere in the world.

The experience of becoming fully integrated with my own activity taught me a valuable lesson that afternoon. I remember going back up on the roof alone later in the day, after we had finished pulling nails, and sitting quietly while I tried to write down a few notes about the day's work. So much of the physical labor that I had done in my life had seemed to be driven by a kind of anger, an urgency to be done with it, and a need to be in control. Whether cutting weeds, planing a piece of wood, or digging a hole, I seemed to always be on the attack, wanting only to get the job done as quickly as possible. But on the roof that day, something new happened. A most revolutionary thing occurred: I relaxed.

And sitting there aloft that evening, with my pen and notebook in hand, I tried to do the impossible, to articulate what it's like to lose yourself in calmly sustained effort without striving for any spectacular result or achievement. I remember thinking a great deal about how people I knew had often related to their work, whether resenting or enjoying it. And for some reason, I thought of how an artist painting a self-portrait usually does not paint the true positions of his hands. Instead of portraying his hands holding a brush and palette, he may represent his hands as relaxed and unmoving. The overall illusion is that the artist is at ease rather than working intently. In a manner of speaking, every bit of work that we do, every tiny facet of our lives, is our own self-portrait. The tools are not important to the end result.

A few weeks later, I found myself in quite a different situation. A leaking water pipe necessitated my crawling underneath our house. Everything I had learned while up on the roof was lost. I had taken one of these crawling excursions before, on my belly, pulling myself along by my hands and elbows, through the impossibly low, damp, scorpion-ridden, and oppressive darkness of the world between the underfloor of the house and the ground. Although I'm not claustrophobic, I remembered feeling nothing but dread as I had squeezed myself into this horrific crawl space the previous time. The idea of having the entire house sitting on top of me made me sweat.

At times like these, I find it helpful to have a large bag of tricks or tools at my disposal, from which I pull out the one illusion in my thinking that will make all of this bearable. In short order, I reasoned that the house had been standing for several decades and would be very unlikely to collapse simply because I happened to be beneath it. The house had better things to do. I tried to bolster my courage by reminding myself how lucky I was to have never had to earn my livelihood by hauling iron ore from mines deep in the earth. I considered the "tunnel rats" of Vietnam. I thought of spelunkers engaged in cave exploration. But this led to memories regarding the terrestrial habitats of venomous spiders and centipedes, and I was not greatly heartened by recovering this knowledge.

I tried to remember the pleasure and insight that I had gained while up on the roof. And I would have liked to be able to report that this somehow worked to assuage all my fear and ease the burden of performing such a distasteful job. But it didn't turn out that way, not this time. It was necessary, this time, to start all over again from scratch. I donned heavy overalls, gloves, and woolen hat, and took my flashlight and pipe wrench and sat down outside the small opening that led to the netherworld. The hidden fangs and the rusted points of overhead nails were waiting.

I looked up into the quiet outside air and wondered: Where are those gentle breezes now? Where is the great insight that came to me while I was on the roof? What happened to all my feelings of sunny resolve and serene well-being? I sat there for quite some time until I remembered that the answers to all of these questions seemed to have something to do with getting on with the work at hand. So once again, I looked up into the air, took the longest, deepest breath I could, and headed down into the darkness.

PART FIVE

Living Arrangements

From another room,

as the sun is descending,

the click of a lamp.

On Living Alone

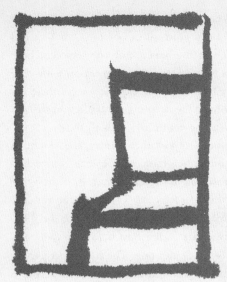

To study Zen is to study ourselves, often in the midst of paradox. Among other contradictions, teachers tell us that we are always alone, that we are never alone, and that both of these statements are true.

In a way, living alone is not something you can ever do by yourself; in another sense, living by yourself is all there ever is. If you find yourself living apart from others, this can be a great opportunity for you to create your own independent path and to fashion your own destiny, learning the differences between solitude and loneliness and between solitude and community.

Did you know that in the animal kingdom, those who choose to live alone are often viewed with particular interest? These "single-minded" animals include a wide range of creatures, from the solitary vireo to the hermit crab. Even species like the wolf, which is usually social and lives in packs, produce "dispersals" or "lone wolves." Whether this choice is deliberate or made for them by others, they follow a path of independent exploration and individual resolve.

People, too, are sometimes drawn toward a life of solitary wandering or to a remote hermitage hidden in the hills. Even those who are most social wish occasionally for space and time alone. There is a deep need, sometimes, to be by ourselves. But are we more "ourselves" when we're alone?

Even when you're alone, you often sense a connection of *some* kind with others. After all, almost none of us can grow all of our food, make all of our clothing, or exist without some of the benefits of our society. There are other factors at work also: You have an ongoing connection with your family, friends, and teachers, as well as with your experiences of the past. Zen practice can be of help in resolving the seeming contradiction that, in every moment of your life, you are alone yet united with all things.

Still, I'm reminded of a recent news report that showed the extent to which a person can be cut off from other humans. German police had discovered the dead body of a man sitting in his apartment, in front of his television set. He had been sitting there *for five years*. The television was still playing, and the lights on the Christmas tree were still shining brightly. The man had decorated the tree five years earlier, just before he died. His neighbors said that he had always been a quiet one. The money to pay his rent and utilities had been automatically withdrawn from his bank account. There had never been a problem, until funds had run low and the landlord had gone knocking on his tenant's door, seeking payment.

The story of this deceased man is an example of a good idea gone too far. Although he was meticulous in not incurring any debt and seemed to be quite self-sufficient, his contact with the world appears to have been limited to what he saw on television. His celebrating Christmas in total isolation is particularly poignant. It makes me wonder if there were gifts under the tree? If so, were they all things he had bought for himself? And I wonder about the last images he saw in his life—those on his television set—the fantasies, documentaries, commercials, and important news events that showered him with flickering rays of electronic light.

Although there are many good reasons for living alone, to attempt to seal yourself off from others in this way is a tragic extreme.

The Zen tradition has always placed great value on self-sufficiency. Traveling monks were often discouraged from settling in or near teaching centers, and were given grueling tests of resolve before they were allowed to enter the temple walls for training. Buddhism in general has always stressed the importance of one's individual quest—the self-questioning and self-examination that occur naturally when one is alone. And Zen in particular has sought to offer students the simplest of frameworks, the most direct ways of letting people discover things for and in themselves.

Yet, at the same time, Zen underscores the interconnectedness of all things and the lack of separation between "self" and "others." It emphasizes to its students the value of working in the community, assisting with hospice, feeding the hungry, and so on. To shut oneself off from others in the manner of the German man would be plainly seen as an act of painful desperation. Even such celebrated monk/poets as Ryokan and Santoka, who were noted for their living and journeying alone, took time along the way to assist others and to play with the village children.

The benefits and pleasures of living independently are many, and need no explanation here. However, if you are ever feeling bewildered by contradiction or beset by indecision regarding living alone, the *Zenrin Kushu* may offer the best advice of all. This book, compiled nearly five centuries ago, suggests that we should always live as though there were others with us; that even when we are alone, we should still "wear our best clothes."

On Living with Others

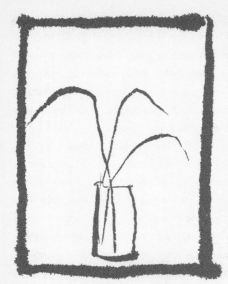

Thich Nhat Hanh uses a wonderful exercise with his students, which you might like to try. Simply look into the palm of your opened hand while attempting to figure out which half of your hand came from your mother and which came from your father. Then try to determine the parts of your hand that came to you from your mother's mother and from your father's father.

The point of this exercise is to examine the conditions of your heritage. Any break in your long line of ancestors would mean that you wouldn't exist, and you owe a profound debt to all those who came before you. Your connection to these family members, as well as your connection to those around you now, never really ends. Also, you're continually influenced by all that is about you; you "inherit" yourself from the rest of the world. Everything in your life is interconnected. All things are one heritage. There are roots and branches, mutations and permutations. But everything is just one whirling, ever-changing family.

When you share your living quarters with others, you gain a greater experience of the world. Rather than just caring for the inanimate objects in your household, you become directly involved in the lives of other people. Whether they're blood relatives, friends, loving companions, or roommates, they provide you with the opportunity to share your life with them. You begin to see parts of yourself in them, and also sense the differences. As you enter different stages in your relationship, you experience the bonds of growing closer, perhaps even older, together. And you find pleasure in your mutual good company, and in the excitement of sharing stories. You pick up on the other person's temperament and realize that communication is of critical importance. You become aware of the subtleties of words.

As Zen has always made clear, there are also subtleties to be found in silence. In the meditation hall, those present are keenly aware of the intimacy that arises when they sit with others in silence. Growling stomachs, throat clearing, sneezes, and whispers are shared by all, and unite the gathered individuals as a single body.

At home, however, this kind of silence is often the result of conflict or heightened tension between occupants. It can be a real challenge to share your home with another. You must breathe the same air, use the same facilities and appliances, and coexist in the same time and space. It's often said that living with others is like putting stones in a tumbler; the stones are rubbed against each other, and their rough and jagged edges are eventually worn smooth. In this way, the stones can settle closer together and show a bit more polish.

So much of what we are has been determined by other people that we sometimes become hidden within the lives of those we live with. We lose our own way and sacrifice or surrender ourselves to this other person or group. In Zen study, we speak of the importance of finding our true nature, the original "self" before we were born. Throughout our lives, we continuously experience change, and at times adopt new friends and family members. We often acquire the traits of others: mannerisms, style, music, language, and knowledge that we make our own.

By living with others, you open yourself to the world of lively interchange, and you're also afforded the opportunity to exercise compassion close at hand. Forgetting yourself for the moment, you yell, "Please pick up your clothes" and "Dinner's ready!"—all in a single breath. Life becomes heightened through shared activity, and as you observe your relationship with others, your own strengths, weaknesses, and intentions become more clearly apparent. This new understanding can be beneficial to you—as well as those you live with—and becomes part of you. It becomes a hand reaching outward, extended toward an even greater household: the family of all things.

On Living with Animal Companions

Dogen said, "If we do not practice with all beings, it is not Buddha's practice." You may ask yourself: Exactly where *are* all of these beings? To find them, you don't have to go far. Researchers have explained that in the event your body should suddenly disappear, a perfect outline of your body, a kind of "living shadow" formed by bacteria and other minute organisms, would still be evident. Our bodies are composed of billions of living and dying cells, and it is difficult to make distinctions between which cells are "us" and which aren't, which are "ours" and which are independent.

Things become clearer when we speak of other animals. The lines are more clearly drawn, and the animals are easier to see. My own childhood experience with pets was a serial adventure of unfortunate, ill-timed, and perplexing encounters with outlaw ant colonies, disappearing budgies, and a dog that could have escaped from Alcatraz without sounding an alarm. Curiously, these encounters led to a lifelong interest in animals, and I've enjoyed their company ever since.

Suzuki Roshi often spoke of the act of bowing to dogs and cats. He felt that it was a very natural thing to do, an act of respect and compassion, a shared moment with another living being.

Buddhist literature, in fact, is filled with references to animals. Countless sutras, Jataka tales, dharma talks, koan collections, and poems refer to horses, dragons, tigers, fish, and birds. Students study Joshu's dog, Nansen's cat, the Oxherding Pictures, and Kanzan's bugs in a bowl. These animals are everywhere: in paradise, hell, and here on Earth. They are always with us, and of that there should be no doubt.

The joy of sharing your home with another creature can be considerable. There is much to be learned from them as you share a relationship that is different from that with your own species. Cross-species communication can be one of the greatest experiences you can have, not to mention the comfort and companionship that your dog, cat, or other pet can provide. The animals' joy in just being what they are is instructive, and perhaps contagious. Doctors say that stroking the fur of a family pet produces heightened feelings of relaxation and well-being. In some cases, patients are encouraged to acquire an animal as an adjunct to other therapies, and positive results are often achieved.

Living with a pet holds some surprises as well. Maybe your dog jumps the fence and runs away, or you live with a cat that refuses to come out of the bookcase. The words *owning, possessing,* and *controlling* become important in these situations. I remember one cold, January morning when breakfast was just being served at our house. My wife and I had both left the kitchen briefly and the table was unattended. When we returned, we found our elderly cat, McKinley, warming herself, seated on a stack of pancakes. Arriving at this comfortable place had taken her a great deal of effort: She had struggled to jump upon a chair and then onto the table itself. After an initial jot of exasperation, I felt a kind of understanding pass between us, and as the ravens outside enjoyed a discarded pancake or two, I marveled at McKinley's alert intensity and lack of self-reproach.

Sometimes, a moment like this stands out from others as being particularly memorable, even when there is no apparent reason to make it so. These moments can be given weight, depending on their context and upon our own ability to clearly perceive them. The wellspring of these moments is ever deep. An acquaintanceship with animals is but one more chance for us to see life's infinite variety, and the many ways its spirit is made visible.

PART SIX

Sweeping Sun, Waxing Moon

We are all haiku—

only here for seventeen

syllables, three lines.

Tinkering with Perfection

One of my grandmothers used to say that doing her housekeeping tasks (reattaching buttons and baking pies, for instance) was as easy as "falling off a bicycle." She was as naturally relaxed and energetic while she worked as any Zen acolyte could ever hope to be.

Still, as students, we try to stay *on* the bicycle. We begin by sitting down (in meditation) and then learn to balance this sitting with self-generated, carefully considered action. In this way, we wobble our way forward, eventually steady ourselves a bit, and ultimately, perhaps, cultivate the capacity to see and experience the world on a more subtle level.

In the spirit of this venturing forward, I would like, from this point onward, to extend our view of home-based Zen practice to include some areas of concern that go beyond the strictly defined perimeters of the dwelling place. For, as our practice deepens, we find more philosophical questions naturally arising, such as issues of time and mortality, a sense of purpose, and the search for perfection.

It is said that a wooden buddha cannot pass through fire, and a clay buddha cannot pass through water. What this means, of course, is that we all have our limits and weaknesses. As Katagiri Roshi said, "Even the Buddhas and the Ancestors can make a mistake." The "human" and ordinary qualities of all buddhas and bodhisattvas are what make them real for us. An ideal that is impossible to realize is useless. There's no point in our striving to become something or someone else. When we recognize and accept who we are, we no longer feel the need to change.

Most of us try to live exemplary lives; we really do try to do our best. But there's no need for us to try to do *better* than our very best. Consider the simple act of washing a coffee cup, for example. When you wash the coffee cup, you do not need to do a perfect job. You do not need to try to make the cup perfect or worry about whether you yourself are perfect. You don't measure the temperature of the water or agonize over the pH balance of the soap. You just wash the cup. If you handle the cup with care, there will be nothing separating you from the cup. There will be no daydreams or distractions, no recriminations, no ideas of self and other, no barriers between you and what you're doing. There will just be washing the cup, and your entire life will be in it.

Looking around, you begin to see the "rightness" of things, the true value they offer. Giving your attention to things costs you nothing, and you have an unlimited quantity of attention to give. You can start by looking at your own hands or at the way the light reflects on the telephone across the room or at the graceful curve of the rubber band resting on your desk. In this way, you can begin to sense the innate peacefulness of things, their reasons for being here, and their transitory nature. As you become more aware of the nuances of the things before you, you gradually come home to your own true self. You begin to identify with the various forces surrounding you and are more ready to accept your place among things. Compassion comes forward to meet you, without your own wild striving, meddling, or interference.

It all sounds so easy, just sitting back and looking at things, but it's very

Tinkering with Perfection

difficult for most of us to do. We're always expecting or wanting something. We are busy trying to find more excitement, more variety, or more volume in our lives. We feel guilty or triumphantly smug about the past. We plot to control and manipulate the future. We wonder who's watching us and what their opinion of us will be. How do we stack up? Is there any chance that someone might know that we're not perfect?

We're terrified that people will find us flawed in some way or that they won't like us because of our imperfections. We sometimes lose sight of who we are, yet we are always our perfect selves. We begin perfectly and we'll end perfectly, regardless of how much we worry about becoming rich or being beautiful or achieving buddhahood.

One should not try too hard to become a buddha. Zen teachers advise us that when we go charging after something, it often eludes us with equal speed. An intense quest for perfection is not ever enough, and perfection itself is not our goal. When we acknowledge that buddhas, at times, declare bankruptcy, get divorced, and fall in the mud, we begin to see perfection in a different light. We understand that buddhas, too, are only human—not much different from ourselves.

On Quiet and Conformity

One early morning at the San Francisco Zen Center, while seated in the formal meditation posture, I had a sudden realization. I realized with absolute certainty that I was the only one present, among the forty or so students in the zendo, who had ever tap-danced in a hotel elevator with James Baldwin and Tennessee Williams. And I was also fairly certain that I was the only one there who had ever climbed down the face of Hoover Dam.

Sitting there on the black cushion, staring at the unadorned wall, I took no particular pride in either of these events and found it quite surprising that these two memories would reveal themselves in that pervasive silence. The people around me undoubtedly had their own unique stories and recollections, and I wondered if others in the meditation hall were recalling interesting narratives of their own. Then the silence took over, and I was once again quieted and unconcerned with past or future, at least for the moment.

What is this nearly incessant narration that keeps going through our heads? It seems that whatever we are doing, wherever we are, we have this little friend with us, who points out things that we should attend to; evaluates, edits, and makes value judgments; refreshes our memories; tries to entertain us and make life more interesting; and infiltrates both our most mundane and our most private thoughts.

It's easy to lose yourself in random conjecturing, especially while working quietly. Thinking washes over you and carries you away. But you lose touch with the crowning immediacy of your life, and any happiness you experience becomes transient and artificial. Try to keep your feet solidly beneath you and your mind restfully aware. When your thoughts begin to drift off, gently try to bring your mind back to the present. This can be very much like standing in the shallow surf, allowing the ocean tide to rush in and back out again without letting yourself be carried away by it.

Strangely, when you're able to quiet the interference of your own thinking, you become more mindful, not less. Rather than shutting yourself off from things, you're able to see them more clearly and experience them with more intensity. When you learn to appreciate the focus that quiet can bring, you may be better prepared to handle a sudden maelstrom of activity and may be less likely to attempt to do everything at once. You'll be able to respond decisively rather than waste time pursuing a variety of unproductive options.

The collective atmosphere of the Zen meditation hall is well arranged and ordered, yet each one sitting there is an individual with his or her own story. The traditional forms of meditation are used for good reason, but not so that students will become like everyone else or even like their teachers. Suzuki Roshi once told a group of his students that it was only after they had all shaved their heads and put on identical black robes that he could truly begin to tell them apart. When people begin to lose their unnecessary affectations, their own individuality is given an opportunity to emerge. Their plain directness reveals the many ways in which they're unique.

Meditating in silence is a little like donning black robes. You turn off your internal music and distracting narrative, and stop worrying about whether you fit in. You realize that stillness can offer another way of learning and communication. Rather than marching to a different drummer, you walk along quietly at your own pace, not leading, not following, just trying to experience the entire parade.

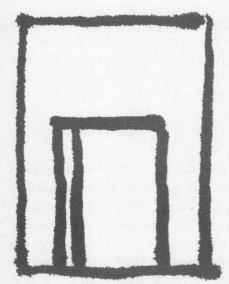

Prayer in Our Practice

There is a marvelous passage in John Muir's book *The Mountains of California* where he describes a harrowing experience that occurred during his climb of Mount Ritter, just outside the eastern border of Yosemite National Park:

The tried dangers beneath seemed even greater than that of the cliff in front; therefore, after scanning its face again and again, I began to scale it, picking my holds with intense caution.

After gaining a point about half way to the top, I was suddenly brought to a dead stop, with arms outspread, clinging close to the face of the rock, unable to move hand or foot either up or down. My doom appeared fixed. I *must* fall. There would be a moment of bewilderment, and then a lifeless rumble down the one general precipice to the glacier below. When this final danger flashed upon me, I became nerve-shaken for the first time since setting foot on the mountain, and my mind seemed to fill with a stifling smoke. But this terrible eclipse lasted only a moment, when life blazed forth again with preternatural clearness. I seemed suddenly to become possessed of a new sense. The other self, bygone experiences, Instinct, or Guardian Angel, call it what you will, came forward and assumed control. Then my trembling muscles became firm again, every rift and flaw in the rock was seen as through a microscope, and my limbs moved with a positiveness and precision with which I seemed to have nothing at all to do. Had I been borne aloft upon wings, my deliverance could not have been more complete.

When your car is going into a skid, when you watch the stack of dishes slowly begin to topple from the tray, when the envelope containing the test results arrives in the mail, and when you're stuck on the mountain, there is that instant when, whether it is voiced or not, a desperate wish for outside help flashes across your consciousness. You're momentarily unable to handle the situation alone and seek something, at least some modicum of assistance, from somewhere outside yourself. Haven't we all had this feeling of being stuck, when it seems impossible for us to go either forward or backward, right or left? What do we do? To whom do we pray, or to whom do we holler for help?

People who are curious about Buddhism sometimes ask whether Buddhists pray, and whether prayer has any place in Zen study. The preeminent Zen scholar D. T. Suzuki (1870–1966) once told a group of people that prayer was completely useless, that everyone was on their own, that there was no one or no thing to pray to, that the entire concept was a ridiculous waste of time. "Of course," he added, "we all do it."

Whether or not you believe in prayer or in some kind of "supreme being," you have a reserve of energy and ingenuity that is waiting to be tapped when you need it most. When things happen quickly—and you haven't the time to ask, "What do I do now?"—you lift the heavy tree from the camper it has fallen upon. Your senses race with awareness; you become focused on what needs to be done. This is more than a simple matter of adrenaline. Each day of your life, you accomplish the impossible. Every day, you conquer one kind of mountain or another.

There are inevitably times when you become stuck, too afraid or too confused to move. But once the crisis has passed, you may marvel at the fact that somehow you have moved beyond the problem. Things *do* become unstuck and begin to flow again, even when most obstructed.

All of us have experienced times when it seems impossible even to maintain our lives, to expend all this effort in decision making and travail. We want more. We want a way out. We want help. And then, suddenly, we seem to pick ourselves up again, to find a foothold where we can dig in and move on. (As Samuel Beckett said, "I can't go on. I'll go on.") The source of this change is, in its own way, quite remarkable; this supplemental surge of tenacity and spirit that rests within us and that comes when we most need it. Whatever it is seems to be firmly in place and available to us only for the asking. Perhaps that's all we seek when we search for the solutions to our questions and the answers to our prayers.

Prayer in Our Practice

Finding Zen, Catching Zen, Holding Zen

The zendo bell has struck, and I sit on my black cushion, feeling for the moment like a cornered beast, being confronted directly by no one thing or person other than myself. There's no escaping the predicament I'm in for at least the next forty minutes. I am obliged to those around me not to move even slightly. I can make no sound. There is no form of rescue available. For the next forty minutes, I might as well be dead, and, in fact, that is the whole idea: to die there and yet remain alert, to see without any thought of body or mind.

Dogen said, "When you take your boat, alone, for miles out onto the ocean, you may see the curvature of the horizon and then believe the ocean to be round. But the ocean is neither round nor square. It has infinite characteristics and boundless virtues."

When you put yourself on the cushion, you are leaving much of your familiar world behind, and opening yourself to whatever new vistas may appear. You are willing to look at whatever comes into view, the infinite characteristics and boundless virtues that form the nature of your reality.

Why do we Zen Buddhists do this? And what caused us to be drawn to the study of Zen Buddhism in the first place? Buddhism is a nonproselytizing religion and philosophy, and even though it has never advertised for or recruited new converts, it has never lacked followers. In theory, it offers the teachings freely to anyone who requests them, but it has never imposed itself upon or tried to interfere with other people's beliefs. For me, its take-it-or-leave-it approach was always part of its attraction. I could devote as much or as little time to it as I wanted. I was in no way coerced and was not presented with even one sugarcoated promise. I was warmly given help when I asked for it, but it was made clear to me that I had to ask. No one was going to come looking for me or come flying overhead to make certain that I hadn't drifted off course. It was up to me to decide the direction in which I wanted to navigate and how quickly I wanted to travel.

Many of my friends, some of whom have devoted decades to serious Zen study, told me their initial interest in Buddhism had been sparked by the casual reading of a magazine article or book. Some had learned about it while taking a college course in Asian history or philosophy. Others had first heard of Zen through friends. Still others had become interested in it while experimenting with drugs, coping with an illness, practicing yoga or other body work, or after seeing the many masterful works of calligraphy, painting, sculpture, and poetry associated with Zen. I've always found it very moving that in the formal meditation halls, or zendos, there are rows of people sitting silently and uniformly in meditation, and that each person represents a different aspect of the same thing—all there for different reasons, from different backgrounds, with different life experiences. The reasons for their coming to Zen practice are sometimes vague. Many people are not so much interested in finding all the answers as they are in determining, at least, whether or not there *are* any answers.

The early teachers referred to this questioning, curiosity, and attraction toward further study as "way-seeking mind," the innate natural desire to come forward and experience one's own buddhahood. Sometimes this way-seeking mind appears to people only briefly or not at all. It may come and go, depending on one's own circumstances. Or it may strongly shape and direct the course of one's entire future. Way-seeking mind is clearly evident in those who pursue Zen study diligently, who question the meaning behind things, and who have a thirst to experience some of these answers directly, without a great deal of talking or intervention. Above all else, Zen is a method of experiencing things. For all of its use of words and ritual, for all of its long tradition of teachings and stories and its history and lineage, Zen is most of all about trying to help us to become grounded in *this moment!*

Whether you study formally in a great temple, informally with a couple of friends, or alone by reading a book at home, you are warned time and time again not to confuse the finger pointing to the moon with the moon itself, not to confuse the teaching with the experience itself. Teachers will try to give you an indication of what is vital in your course of study, but it is up to you, individually, to try to discern the differences between the teaching and the essence of what is being taught. You learn in the beginning that if you aren't confused, you are probably not really trying. And the older students will tell you that they're the ones who have been confused the longest. You hope that this has been uttered, at least somewhat, with tongue in cheek.

All of Zen seems to be pointing you in the right direction, and you are told that the breeze in the hedge, the cloud of smoke coming from the rear of the bus, and the peeling posters on the abandoned wall are all signposts showing you the way things are. "Look! Look!" you are told. "It's right there in front of you!" Zen is not a discovery or an experience that happens somewhere else. It's not, necessarily, waiting for you in a faraway temple or monastery. Dogen Zenji asked his students, "If you cannot find the truth right here where you are, where can you ever expect to find it?"

We grow up thinking that we know all about things. And we believe that if there's something important we don't know, we'll learn it as we go along. We learn how to make soup and how to behave at parties. We learn to be discerning, to distinguish between good and bad, to know what we like and what we find objectionable. But our knowledge sometimes confuses us. There are different kinds of knowledge. Knowledge acquired by touching something with our hands, for example, is different from theoretical learning and abstract reasoning. The reality of dreams is quite unlike the reality of cleaning the refrigerator. We wonder what things really are, or what a certain event really means, and we try to glimpse a purpose behind each encounter. We see many indications of deeper meaning in our lives but fail to follow them to any real conclusion.

The finger that points toward the moon is near, but the moon seems very far away. Zen teachers assure us that the light of the moon is everywhere. Opportunities for discovering this moonlight are endless, but they must be rooted in personal experience rather than any outside source.

If you want to learn to swim, you must first enter the water. You can talk to people who have *gone* swimming and study the scientific characteristics of water; you can practice overhead arm movements, work on holding your breath, and invest in a brand-new swimsuit. But nothing compares to actually plunging into the water—where you can feel *wateriness* to the very root of your being. You then "experience" water and know it in a truly different way. You'll never forget it. You'll always be able to relate to it, even though you may have difficulty describing it in words.

Unlike the "revealed" religions that offer scripture, teaching, or pronouncement from a "higher" or more "heavenly" source, Zen stresses the value of your own engagement in your own experience. It teaches that the last words the Buddha spoke were calls to "work out your own salvation with diligence." On the face of it, this is much more than just daunting. It is catastrophic. "Good luck," the Buddha says, and then kicks you out of the leaking boat, leaving it to you to either sink or swim on your own.

But as you calm down, you see that things aren't quite so desperate as they at first seemed. In fact, you realize that the very Buddha that made that statement trusts you and has absolute confidence in your abilities. There's no reason to gloss things over, no hint of mollycoddling, no promising you the moon. "I did it," the Buddha seems to say, "and so can you."

So each one of us comes to this practice somewhat prepared for the adventure of saving ourselves from our own delusion and ultimate destruction. We have at least a glimmer of the way-seeking mind. We have a human life that is ours to experience, and we have a limitless universe of other beings to whom we can offer our help and who help us in return. All we have to do is jump into the waters of our life and join in—entering the swim of things.

A Question of Time

One day last week, I sat down and tried to figure out how I could do five hours' worth of work in just three hours. Most of us continually try to fit too many things into time's small container. From our birth onward, we are at the mercy of those two strict taskmasters, the clock and the calendar—both of which are thoroughly arbitrary and artificial in concept. There is nothing more real than the time we have between our birth and death, but this time is not in any way related to the positions of the two hands of the clock. As social animals, we have found it easier to categorize our lives into seconds, minutes, days, years, Junes, Julys, winters, leap years, and holidays. We meet at two o'clock for lunch. We pick the kids up at four. We go to the seashore in August. And we'll take the garbage out in a few minutes.

Many of us have abused time throughout our lives by trying to turn it into something it's not. We have pasted wings on it and pretended that, even though it flies, it is under our control. We seem obsessed with trying to drive our lives this way and that, much as we steer an automobile. We study time-management and enter into time-sharing. We work full-time or part-time, and after work we try to find time to have a good time. Our preoccupation with time would undoubtedly qualify as a psychological fixation, if not for the fact that nearly everyone is preoccupied with it. As members of society, we are determined not only to stay alive forever but to stay *young* forever, dreading the day we might ever become obsolete or go out of fashion.

Every other creature on Earth and every plant functions in the present. We humans are the only ones who fret about what hour it is, who try to strap some controlling measure of time onto our wrists, and who hang a reminder of the coming days on our walls. Other life-forms seem to have no difficulty recognizing when it's time to eat, time to run, time to build a nest, or time to go up to the surface and take a breath of air. Animals always seem to know what to do. They seldom seem to be at loose ends.

Let's try doing something really radical. For just an hour, try to free yourself from time's invisible shackles. Do a few things and spend as long as it takes to complete them. Don't worry about how long it takes to write a friend a letter. Or how long it takes to go for a walk or clean out the refrigerator. Let things happen in their own time.

Of course, you can always set limits for yourself and say that you'll write a letter and go for a short walk and toss out the wilted lettuce and be done in time for the six o'clock news. But then you're not really living your life; you're being expeditious and hurried, scheduled and prompt. It might be better to leave the news and the lettuce until later and just write the letter to your friend, taking as much time as you need.

When you see a photograph of yourself as a child, you know that the child in the picture has grown into who you are; but do you realize that, in the instant the photograph was taken, the child you were had already become someone else? The camera does not stop time. It can only offer souvenirs, reference points to places traveled along the way.

There is a classic Zen koan that asks you to describe your own original face, the one you had before you were born. I've never come as close to being able to answer that question as I did the year my mother died. She had cancer and became bedridden for a very short time. During the last three or four days of her life, she began to change outwardly a great deal. She lost weight rapidly, and her skin began to tighten and become less wrinkled. She, in fact, began to appear transformed into someone very relaxed and quite young. She began to closely resemble the old photos of her that I had seen, pictures taken when she was in her early twenties. She was like a young woman who had dyed her hair gray, as if on a whim—a restless echo of happier times.

When I looked at her, I felt swallowed up in some kind of enormous gift. It was as if I had been given the opportunity of seeing my mother as she was before I was born. Time seemed to stand still. And time became exceptionally real for me, only because it ceased to exist. The woman before me was time. And I was time. And the room was time.

George Bernard Shaw (who lived to be ninety-four) once offered the following succinct advice: "Do not try to live forever. You will not succeed." Managing time is not the important thing. What you're doing and how you're doing it are what matter. Every event happens in its own time. The mother cat moves her kittens to a safer place. A man in Kansas washes his car. And in the Arctic fringes, a chunk of glacial ice falls into the sea. Each action is the result of what has gone on before it. The events in your life happen this way also, occurring just when it's time for them to happen, just when they become ripe. The kind of seeds you plant now in your life will determine what comes later. As my grandmother used to say, "The seed just keeps filling with its own life, and grows—even if it never sees the finished flower."

The One Who Listens

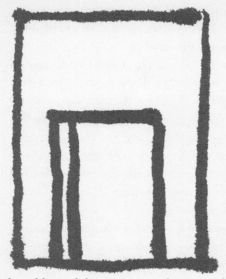

Near the open door of Zen Center's dining room, someone has swept together a mixed pile of dust, grit, crumbs, and sunlight. Only by the broom following a dozen varying paths was this convergence achieved. The sunlight seems to spill forward and flow across the floor like water. And in my imagination, I envision Sahasrabhujavalokitesvara, another manifestation of the thousand-armed Kannon, holding a broom in each of her hands and spinning slowly like a waterwheel.

Kannon, or Kanzeon, is the Japanese name for the Buddhist deity Avalokitesvara. This figure is the personification of compassion, the one who hears and sees all the world's suffering. In the Japanese tradition, Kannon is a figure without specific gender; however, most American Buddhists today refer to her as being female. She may have two, four, six, or as many as a thousand arms, and sometimes there is an eye in each of her hands. At other times, her hands hold work tools, household implements, musical instruments, or precious jewels. She can hold whatever you want her to, because many Buddhist teachers believe that we are, each of us, one of her useful appendages; we are the ones who live in the world and hear its suffering and are able to do what we can to help ease it. Kannon is, in her quiet way, one of Buddhism's real heroes; she is a reminder to all who see her that it is important to listen and watch carefully, and to use whatever is at hand to provide aid and develop understanding.

Do you think of yourself as heroic? Do you see any real significance in changing a tire or in bundling together month-old newspapers? Thich Nhat Hanh once wrote in one of his journals: "Washing the dishes and cooking are themselves the path to Buddhahood. . . . Only a person who has grasped the art of cooking, washing dishes, sweeping, and chopping wood, someone who is able to laugh at the world's weapons of money, fame, and power, can hope to descend the mountain as a hero. A hero like that will traverse the waves of success and failure without rising or sinking. In fact, few people will recognize him as a hero at all."

Many people feel that they never even have the opportunity to descend the mountain at all, let alone become heroes. For them, their entire life consists of climbing and striving to reach a higher peak or plateau. And they also see themselves as being buried in an avalanche of unending routine. (But the word *routine* originally meant "a route or course of travel for trading," or "a religious pilgrimage," and has only more recently come to mean "ordinary" or "of no special quality.")

In fact, nothing in your life is ordinary. There is no ordinary breath or heartbeat; there is no ordinary force of gravity; there is no ordinary birth or death. *Natural,* yes—but never ordinary. In a certain sense, just living your life *does* engender a type of courage, especially when you're fully aware of all the others who are in it with you. Listening to your friends is sometimes not that easy to do. Lending someone a hand may interfere with your own ideas of how the day should be spent. This is why Kannon finds herself in garden settings, at crossroads, and ensconced in people's kitchens, all invaluable vantage points for gaining a broader perspective. She is with us as we hear the sounds of the world's suffering, as well as its music and its "routine" sounds of daily life. As we wash our vegetables, she hears the rustling of our actions and comes to our assistance. The work goes easier, and then she's gone. Who knows who the heroes are? Maybe someday each of us will descend the mountain and begin to see the value in all of our sweeping and washing, the open promise of each day.

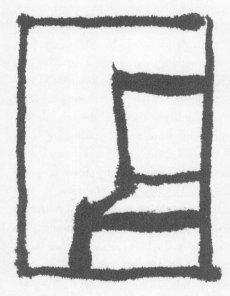

Epilogue: The Buddha in the Bookcase

I was visiting a bookshop, not far from where I live, when a man nervously approached the salesclerk and asked for the kind of help that all booksellers dread: He needed assistance in finding a book whose author, title, and publisher he did not know. "I saw it on television," he said. The salesclerk's face immediately brightened, and he said to the customer, "Please follow me." He then walked briskly to a back corner of the shop and pulled the first book from the topmost shelf. "Is this it?" he asked, showing the book to the customer. And the customer replied that it wasn't. The clerk replaced the book and then chose the one next to it. "Is this it?"

There was no reply. After three attempts, the customer got the message. If he really wanted the book, the clerk would have to search, one book at a time, through the complete inventory of the store. Sometimes we know what we're looking for, but we don't have much to go on.

When I became curious about Buddhism, and Zen in particular, my very first inclination was to head for the bookstore and the library. This was in the late 1950s, and it was an eye-opener and a heart-sinker to learn that there was almost nothing available on either subject, at least in English. Today, the shelves are running over with Zen books. There is no escaping them: Zen and the Internet, Zen and walking, Zen and eating, Zen and golf, Zen and the weather. There are also a great many "I Conquered Zen" books: accounts of how people actually found all the answers to life's mysteries, how they realized their bliss, and how they plumbed the depths of their newly discovered Zen souls. There are serious, scholarly texts. There are even books about Zen and your cat, your canary, and your computer. To keep track of all these Zen books is fast approaching the mapping of the stars in its complexity. (The problem, of course, is that having too many choices is as paralyzing as having none at all.) Selecting books is difficult not only for a person who is just becoming interested in the subject, but also for those who have studied and read Zen books for decades.

And there is one other small complication. I can vividly recall one glaring sentence in the first book on Zen I ever read: "Zen does not rely on the study of words or letters." Well, this seemed to be quite obvious. Zen is not about having a reading experience. So where do books, consisting solely of many thousands of words and letters, fit into all of this?

The question really revolves around what is meant by *dharma*. This word exemplifies what is known as the "truth" of Buddhist teachings. Originally, these teachings were recognized as being only the words spoken by the Buddha himself. They usually took the form of sutras, long transcriptions of sermons and related materials that the Buddha offered to his followers. Naturally, throughout the millennia that followed, these words of Buddha were altered, expanded, reinterpreted, sometimes lost and rediscovered, and were revered by some and found suspect by others.

As with many terms, today's definition of *dharma* has been broadened. It now includes a great many other teachings. In fact, the much-revered Lotus Sutra tells us that "all things, at all times, offer Buddha's teachings and preach the *dharma*." Longtime followers of Zen realize that nothing can be left out. An interview with a teacher, a poem, or a brief conversation can be of significant value. And as long as reading is not the exclusive method of study, it can be quite helpful. There is no substitute for *zazen*, or meditation, or for sharing in work-practice with others, but reading often answers questions, removes mystery, and offers camaraderie to people who are studying on their own. For many of us in the early days, it was indispensable.

The books we choose to read will often reflect other areas of interest that we might have. There are excellent collections of Zen-inspired poetry that are widely available. Most notable among them are the wonderful translations of and lively commentary on haiku poetry and related subjects by R. H. Blyth. There are also good, strong translations of works by the monk-poet Ryokan (see Abe, Stevens, Watson, and Yuasa in the bibliography). Beginning students will find many of their questions answered in *Zen Mind, Beginner's Mind* by Shunryo Suzuki Roshi. Two early books by Robert Aitken, *Taking the Path of Zen* and *The Mind of Clover,* are also especially valuable for beginners.

Readers new to Zen literature often find it helpful to read slowly and to try to absorb the words as they appear on the page. Don't be distracted by wondering whether another book might be better—whether you might understand things more quickly with another writer or whether the real answers might be over there rather than here. I have read some of the basic texts time after time, and always find something new in them. Remember that Zen has to come from your own experience, not the experiences of others. But careful reading can give you a gentle push and put you on the right track.

Over the years, I've read many useful and enjoyable books about Buddhism and Zen. Among my favorites are the books by Robert Aitken, D. T. Suzuki, and Zen master Dogen (particularly the collections edited by Kazuaki Tanahashi and those of Francis Cook). I would also recommend anything translated by Thomas Cleary, and the remarkable history of Buddhism in America titled *How the Swans Came to the Lake,* by Rick Fields. Any of the many books by Thich Nhat Hanh would be most valuable, as would those by Gary Snyder, Burton Watson, and John Stevens. Natalie Goldberg does an expert job with the subject of Zen and writing, and Edward Espe Brown's books on Zen and cooking are entertaining and instructive.

Of course, these are only a few of the many books available. It's up to you to do some sleuthing on your own. See what appeals to you and try to ascertain why some of them seem more interesting to you than others. It's just as important for you to know your own desires and motivations as it is for you to select the right book or pursue a certain course of study.

Also keep in mind that a great deal of dharma is to be found even in books written by people who have never heard of the Z-word. Cookbooks and gardening books, the works of scientists, psychologists, and writers of natural history, children's books, and auto-repair manuals, all teach the dharma in their own fashion. They show us things that we would not otherwise know. They instruct us on how to care for things. They teach us how to remove a bolt without scraping all the skin from our knuckles, how to deal with caterpillars, how to find a long-distance telephone number, and how to prepare a meal that won't alienate our friends. These authors try to enlighten us and keep us out of trouble. What could be more Zenlike than that?

A Selected Bibliography
for Further Reading on Zen,
Japanese Culture, and Related Matters

Abe, Ryuichi, and Peter Haskel. *Great Fool: Zen Master Ryokan*. Honolulu: University of Hawaii Press, 1996.

Aitken, Robert. *Encouraging Words*. New York: Pantheon Books, 1993.

———. *The Gateless Barrier*. San Francisco: North Point Press, 1990.

———. *The Mind of Clover*. San Francisco: North Point Press, 1984.

———. *Original Dwelling Place*. Washington, D.C.: Counterpoint, 1996.

———. *The Practice of Perfection*. New York: Pantheon Books, 1994.

———. *Taking the Path of Zen*. San Francisco: North Point Press, 1982.

Anderson, Tenshin Reb. *Warm Smiles from Cold Mountains*. San Francisco: San Francisco Zen Center, 1995.

App, Urs. *Master Yunmen*. New York: Kodansha, 1994.

Austin, James H., M. D. *Zen and the Brain*. Cambridge, Mass.: MIT Press, 1998.

Blyth, R. H. *Edo Satirical Verse Anthologies*. Tokyo: Hokuseido Press, 1961.

———. *The Genius of Haiku*. Tokyo: Hokuseido Press, 1995.

———. *Haiku*. 4 vols. Tokyo: Hokuseido Press, 1949–52.

———. *Zen in English Literature and Oriental Classics*. Tokyo: Hokuseido Press, 1942.

Brown, Edward Espe. *The Tassajara Bread Book*. Boston: Shambhala Publications, 1970.

———. *Tassajara Cooking*. Boston: Shambhala Publications, 1973.

————. *Tomato Blessings and Radish Teachings*. New York: Riverhead Books, 1997.

Callicott, J. Baird, and Roger T. Ames. *Nature in Asian Traditions of Thought.* Albany, N.Y.: State University of New York Press, 1989.

Carter, Steven D. *Traditional Japanese Poetry.* Stanford: Stanford University Press, 1991.

Chadwick, David. *Crooked Cucumber: The Life and Zen Teachings of Shunryu Suzuki.* New York: Broadway Books, 1999.

————. *Thank You and OK! An American Zen Failure in Japan.* New York: Penguin, Arkana, 1994.

Cleary, Thomas. *The Blue Cliff Record.* Revised ed. Boston: Shambhala Publications, 1992.

————. *Book of Serenity.* Hudson, N.Y.: Lindisfarne Press, 1990.

————. *Rational Zen: The Mind of Dogen Zenji.* Boston: Shambhala Publications, 1992.

————. *Shobogenzo: Zen Essays by Dogen.* Honolulu: University of Hawaii Press, 1986.

————. *Timeless Spring: A Soto Zen Anthology.* Tokyo: Weatherhill, 1980.

Cook, Francis H. *How to Raise an Ox.* Los Angeles: Center Publications, 1978.

————. *Sounds of the Valley Streams.* Albany, N.Y.: State University of New York Press, 1989.

Dogen, Eihei, and Koshu Uchiyama Roshi. *From the Zen Kitchen to Enlightenment.* New York: Weatherhill, 1983.

Fields, Rick. *How the Swans Came to the Lake.* Revised ed. Boston: Shambhala Publications, 1992.

Foster, Nelson, and Jack Shoemaker. *The Roaring Stream: A New Zen Reader.* Hopewell, N.J.: Ecco Press, 1996.

Goldberg, Natalie, *Wild Mind: Living the Writer's Life*. New York: Bantam Books, 1990.

——. *Writing Down the Bones: Freeing the Writer Within*. Boston: Shambhala Publications, 1986.

Heine, Steven. *A Blade of Grass: Japanese Poetry and Aesthetics in Dogen Zen*. New York: Peter Lang, 1989.

——. *Dogen and the Koan Tradition*. Albany, N.Y.: State University of New York Press, 1994.

Hirota, Dennis. *Wind in the Pines: Classic Writings of the Way of Tea as a Buddhist Path*. Fremont, Calif.: Asian Humanities Press, 1995.

Inagaki, Hisao. *A Glossary of Zen Terms*. Kyoto: Nagata Bunshodo, 1991.

Kaplinski, Jaan. *The Wandering Border*. Port Townsend, Wash.: Copper Canyon Press, 1987.

Katagiri, Dainin. *Returning to Silence: Zen Practice in Daily Life*. Boston: Shambhala Publications, 1988.

——. *You Have to Say Something; Manifesting Zen Insight*. Boston: Shambhala Publications, 1998.

Kim, Hee-jin. *Dogen Kigen, Mystical Realist*. Revised ed. Tucson: University of Arizona Press, 1987.

Kraft, Kenneth. *Zen: Tradition and Transition*. New York: Grove Press, 1988.

La Fleur, William R., ed. *Dogen Studies*. Honolulu: University of Hawaii Press, 1985.

Leighton, Taigen Daniel. *Bodhisattva Archetypes*. New York: Penguin, Arkana, 1998.

——. *Cultivating the Empty Field: The Silent Illumination of Hongzhi*. San Francisco: North Point Press, 1991.

——. *Dogen's Pure Standards for the Zen Community*. Albany, N.Y.: State University of New York Press, 1996.

Lowenstein, Tom. *The Vision of the Buddha*. London: Macmillan, 1996.

Maezumi, Hakuyu Taizan, and Bernard Glassman. *On Zen Practice*. 2 vols. Los Angeles: Zen Center of Los Angeles, 1976–77.

Masunaga, Reiho. *A Primer of Soto Zen*. London: Routledge and Kegan Paul, 1972.

Matthiessen, Peter. *Nine-Headed Dragon River: Zen Journals, 1969–1982*. Boston: Shambhala Publications, 1986.

Miura, Isshu, and Ruth Fuller Sasaki. *Zen Dust*. New York: Harcourt Brace, 1966.

Nhat Hanh, Thich. *Interbeing: Fourteen Guidelines for Engaged Buddhism*. Berkeley: Parallax Press, 1987.

———. *Present Moment Wonderful Moment*. Berkeley: Parallax Press, 1990.

———. *Fragrant Palm Leaves: Journals 1962–1966*. Berkeley: Parallax Press, 1998.

Nishimima, Gudo, trans. *Shinji Shobogenzo*. Woods Hole, Mass.: Windbell Publications, 1990.

Nishijima, Gudo, and Chodo Cross. *Shobogenzo*. 4 vols. London: Windbell Publications, 1994–99.

Omori, Sogen. *An Introduction to Zen Training*. London: Kegan Paul, 1996.

Sakaki, Nanao. *Break the Mirror*. San Francisco: North Point Press, 1987.

Sanford, James, William LaFleur, and Masatoshi Nagatomi, eds. *Flowing Traces: Buddhism in the Literary and Visual Arts of Japan*. Princeton, N.J.: Princeton University Press, 1992.

Sato, Hiroaki, and Burton Watson. *From the Country of Eight Islands*. Seattle: University of Washington Press, 1981.

Sekida, Katsuki. *Two Zen Classics: Mumonkan and Hekiganroku*. New York: Weatherhill, 1977.

Shibayama, Zenkei. *Zen Comments on the Mumonkan*. New York: Harper and Row, 1974.

Shigematsu, Soiku. *A Zen Forest*. New York: Weatherhill, 1991.

————. *A Zen Harvest*. San Francisco: North Point Press, 1988.

Shimano, Eido, ed. *Like a Dream, Like a Fantasy: The Zen Writings and Translations of Nyogen Senzaki*. Tokyo: Japan Publications, 1978.

Snyder, Gary. *Earth House Hold*. New York: New Directions, 1969.

————. *No Nature: New and Selected Poems*. New York: Pantheon Press, 1992.

————. *A Place in Space: Ethics, Aesthetics, and Watersheds*. Washington, D.C.: Counterpoint, 1995.

————. *The Practice of the Wild*. San Francisco: North Point Press, 1990.

————. *The Real Work: Interviews and Talks, 1964–1979*. New York: New Directions, 1980.

Stambaugh, Joan. *Impermanence Is Buddha-Nature: Dogen's Understanding of Temporality*. Honolulu: University of Hawaii Press, 1990.

Stevens, John. *Mountain Tasting: Zen Haiku by Santoka Taneda*. New York: Weatherhill, Inc., 1980.

————. *One Robe, One Bowl: The Zen Poetry of Ryokan*. New York: Weatherhill, Inc., 1977.

Suzuki, Daisetz T. *The Essentials of Zen Buddhism*. New York: Dutton, 1962.

————. *The Outlines of Mahayana Buddhism*. New York: Schocken Books, 1963.

————. *Zen and Japanese Culture*. Princeton, N.J.: Princeton University Press/Bollingen Foundation, 1959.

Suzuki, Shunryu. *Zen Mind, Beginner's Mind*. New York: Weatherhill, 1970.

Tanahashi, Kazuaki, ed. *Enlightenment Unfolds: The Essential Teachings of Zen Master Dogen*. Boston: Shambhala Publications, 1999.

————. *Moon in a Dewdrop: Writings of Zen Master Dogen*. San Francisco: North Point Press, 1985.

Tanahashi, Kazuaki, and Tensho David Schneider, eds. *Essential Zen*. San Francisco: HarperCollins, 1994.

Thurman, Robert A. F. *Essential Tibetan Buddhism*. San Francisco: Harper-Collins, 1995.

Tonkinson, Carole, ed. *Wake Up and Cook: Kitchen Buddhism in Words and Recipes*. New York: Riverhead Books, 1997.

Tucker, Mary Evelyn, and Duncan Ryuken Williams, ed. *Buddhism and Ecology*. Cambridge, Mass.: Harvard University Center for the Study of World Religions, 1997.

Tworkov, Helen. *Zen in America: Profiles of Five Zen Teachers*. San Francisco: North Point Press, 1989.

Uchiyama, Kosho. *Opening the Hand of Thought*. New York: Penguin, Arkana, 1993.

Ueda, Makoto. *Basho and His Interpreters*. Stanford: Stanford University Press, 1991.

Watson, Burton. *Ryokan: Zen Monk-Poet of Japan*. New York: Columbia University Press, 1977.

Wenger, Michael. *Thirty-three fingers: A Collection of Modern American Koans*. San Francisco: Clear Glass Publishing, 1994.

White, Jonathan, ed. *Talking on the Water: Conversations About Nature and Creativity*. San Francisco: Sierra Club Books, 1994.

Yamada, Koun. *Gateless Gate*. Tucson: University of Arizona Press, 1979.

Yanagi, Sori, ed. *The Woodblock and the Artist: The Life and Work of Shiko Munakata*. Tokyo: Kodansha, 1991.

Yasutani, Hakuun. *Flowers Fall: A Commentary on Zen Master Dogen's Genjokoan*. Boston: Shambhala Publications, 1996.

Yuasa, Nobuyuki. *The Zen Poems of Ryokan*. Princeton, N.J.: Princeton University Press, 1981.

Zen Studies Society. *Soen Roku: The Sayings and Doings of Master Soen*. New York: Zen Studies Society Press, 1986.

———. *Sutra Book*. New York: Zen Studies Society Press, 1982.

Subject Index

Doors   11–12, 13
Dust, dusting   18, 19–21

Eating   66–69

Emptiness, form and   22–31
Enlightened mind, mirror representing   93
Existence, transitory nature of   50, 74
Experience   135–37, 146

Family   118, 120

Fashion   41
Fire   80–82
Food   64–65, 66–69, 90
Form, and emptiness   22–31
Furnishings   41, 42–43, 44

Happiness   29–30

Heat   77, 78, 80, 81
Heritage, examining conditions of   118
Home   xvi, 1–2, 6, 28, 43–44, 45
   furnishings   42–43
   maintaining   34–38, 48
   places of homage in   53–56
   sharing with animals   121–22
   smallest rooms in   88–92

Impermanence   34–35, 38, 45, 50

Insects   72–74, 76
Integrative practice   91

Laundry xiii, 91–92
Lawns 105–6
Letting go 6, 29, 51, 102, 104
Life 3, 63, 64, 85–86, 87, 122, 142
Light 32, 33–34, 108–11
Literature, Zen 5, 11, 121, 145–46
Living alone 115–17
Living with animal companions 120–22
Living with others 118–20

Maintenance 4, 34–38, 48, 78
Meaning 5, 52, 136
Meditation (*zazen*) 2, 3, 4, 6, 57, 78, 81, 91, 94, 134, 145
  sitting 2, 4, 91, 125
  thoughts interfering with 128–29
  traditional forms of 129–30
Mirrors 93–95
Moment (the) 3, 35, 135
Moon, full 104
Moving stone 106–8

Nonduality 77–78
Nonthinking 39

Objects 26, 27, 44–45; *see also* Things
Observation 27
Outside tasks 101–8
Oven, cleaning 79–80

Painting 38–40
Perfection 7, 125–27

GARY THORP began studying Zen in 1960 and was later lay-ordained in the lineage of Shunryu Suzuki Roshi. A former bookseller and jazz pianist, he is a full-time writer, doing research in marine biology and the ecology of mountain lions. He lives with his wife, Lura, in Marin County, California.